Group Work Education
in the Field

Strengthening Group Work Education

A Series from the

Council on Social Work Education
and the
Association for the Advancement
of Social Work with Groups

Lawrence Shulman, Series Editor

Volume 2

Group Work Education in the Field

Julianne Wayne and Carol S. Cohen

Council on Social Work Education
Alexandria, VA

To our families for their love and support through it all:
Murray, Lenny, & Raymie—a valued colleague as well—and
Joe, Abie, Charlotte, & Jerry

Library of Congress Cataloging-in-Publication Data

Wayne, Julianne L.
    Group work education in the field / Julianne Wayne & Carol S. Cohen.

        p. cm. — (Strengthening group work education ; v. 2)
    Includes bibliographical references and index.
    ISBN 0-87293-087-4
    1. Social group work – Study and teaching – United States.   I.
Cohen, Carol S., 1950-   . II. Title. III. Series.
    HV45 .W39 2001
    361.4′071′5 – dc21
                                2001003200
Manufactured in the United States of America.

Contents

Series Introduction
Strengthening Group Work Education

This book is the second in a series of three joint publications of the Council on Social Work Education (CSWE) and the Association for the Advancement of Social Work with Groups (AASWG). It is the result of a cooperative effort between CSWE and the AASWG Commission for Strengthening Group Work in Social Work Education. The effort began five years ago and has included the development of a network of faculty liasions across the country who have worked on a local level holding conferences and training programs for interested faculty. Workshops have also been presented at national conferences for social work educators. In this book, Julianne Wayne and Carol Cohen, two outstanding social group work educators, have shared their knowledge and experience in the area of field work by providing an excellent guide for field instructors on integrating group work into the field work experience.

The first book in this series, *Teaching a Methods Course in Social Work with Groups*, on designing and teaching a group work course was authored by Roselle Kurland and Robert Salmon. It has been well received by social work educators and is already in its second printing. Carol and Julianne's book continues in this tradition of providing a quality, practice-focused resource for social work programs.

Lawrence Shulman
Former Chair, AASWG Commission for
Strengthening Group Work in Social Work Education
Dean, School of Social Work
University at Buffalo, State University of New York

Chapter 1 | Introduction

This volume is designed to serve as a resource for group work education in the field. Its purpose is to help field instructors teach students to conceptualize and engage in practice that is informed by knowledge and theory.

Developments in social work education over the years have heightened the need for a resource such as this. In that time, the movement towards a generic perspective of direct practice and away from distinct boundaries between education for work with individuals and work with groups has encouraged professionals to generalize their knowledge and transfer skills from one size client system to the other. While most social workers embrace this phenomenon and believe it is ultimately clients who will benefit from this broadened perspective of service, there is evidence that many practitioners have not acquired all the specialized knowledge and skills required for high quality and effective group work practice. This is understandable. Birnbaum and Auerbach (1994) in their survey of graduate social work education found that "most schools offer group work only as an elective, and few students graduate with a course in this subject" (p. 325). Graduates of most programs rely upon the content of generic practice courses to provide the conceptual foundation for their group work practice. These courses, however, often do not include content that is specific to work with groups. (Birnbaum & Wayne, 2000).

This movement away from specialized group work education has had its impact on field instruction for group work practice. Studies reveal that the group work method is supervised by field instructors who rate their group work skills lower than their casework skills. Further, apprenticeship training, rather than conceptualized education, is more widely used in the teaching of group work than it is in the teaching of casework practice (Wayne & Garland, 1990). For example, Wayne (1988) found that field instructors identified process recordings as a tool for helping students conceptualize practice, while Wayne and Garland (1990) found that they were used in the supervision of cases by 65% of field instructors, and only by 29% in the supervision of work with groups. Most field instructors in this study required no written work of any kind for the supervision of group work practice. In addition, students frequently have co-leadership group work assignments, often with a senior practitioner. In these latter instances, though not necessarily articulated as such, they are expected to learn largely through observation of the "master," yet another apprenticeship approach. While teaching through modeling has its benefits, it has limited effectiveness as the major approach for a professional education designed to help students learn to exercise independent judgement based on the combination of their growing knowledge and sharpening sensitivity.

Contents

The book provides information and materials to increase the effectiveness of group work education in the field. It takes a holistic approach by offering both what to teach and how to teach it. The chapters lay varying emphases on each of these dimensions. While individual chapters can be helpful on their own, they offer different perspectives on shared concepts, which are best understood by reading the book in its entirety.

Following this introduction, Chapter 2 helps students understand the "why" that underlies the "how" of serving members through groups, and provides guidelines for helping students to maximize the special benefits of group membership. Chapter 3 addresses the field instructor self-assessment, and the agency as the context for group work practice, as well as identifying aspects of agency culture, often overlooked, that could either strengthen or weaken group work efforts. Chapter 4 identifies a range of group purposes, types, and models that could serve as field assignments. The special characteristics and educational benefits of each are explored. Chapter 5 offers structures and tools to enhance learning-teaching transactions, including an examination of the parallels between group supervision and group work practice. The range of educational options offered is related to the range of students' learning patterns and phases. Chapter 6 revisits the concept of parallel process by, among other things, encouraging field instructors to tune in to their students' feelings and concerns about working with groups, and encouraging them to do the same in relation to group members' hopes, fears, and feelings of vulnerability about the group experience that lies ahead.

Chapter 7 identifies the factors that must be carefully considered as part of the group planning process. A student placed in a nursing home was once overheard complaining that he would never be able to practice group work because of all the problems he faced in eliciting cooperation from the nursing staff and in recruiting members. These chapters present such challenges as part of, not peripheral to, group work practice and provide guidelines for dealing with them. Chapter 8 focuses on helping students and field instructors to evaluate the group's progress and students' practice.

The professional arena, including social group work, must constantly adapt to meet the emerging needs and challenges of an ever-changing society. Therefore, Chapter 9 completes the book with suggestions to field instructors about how to remain abreast of ongoing developments while deepening their appreciation and understanding of group work practice. Group members can only benefit from such a commitment.

References

Birnbaum, M., & Auerbach, C. (1994). Group work in graduate social work education: The price of neglect. *Journal of Social Work Education*, *30*, 325-335.

Birnbaum, M., & Wayne, J. (2000). Group work content in foundation generalist education: The necessity for change. *Journal of Social Work Education*, *36*, 347-356.

Wayne, J., & Garland, J. (1990). Group work education in the field: The state of the art. *Social Work with Groups*, *13*(2), 95-109.

Wayne, J. (1988). A comparison of beliefs about student supervision between micro and macro practitioners. *The Clinical Supervisor*, *6*(3/4), 271-297.

Chapter 2 | The Special Value of Social Group Work: Implications for Intervention

Before students begin to consider and plan for a group work experience, it would be helpful for them to understand the why that precedes the how. The major motivation for starting a group can be either the recognition of the benefits of peer support for a certain group of clients, or the student's desire to have a group experience, or a school requirement that students have a group experience. The latter reasons, though based more on the student's than the client's needs, are not unimportant. Enthusiasm, interest, and accountability are important motivators. Peer support is a significant and legitimate client-centered reason to use groups, but the phrase "peer support" in and of itself is too general to be of great help in guiding student interventions. In order to capitalize on the value of a group experience, the student must be helped to identify specific contributions to group members that differ from the benefits of one-to-one intervention. With awareness of these factors, the student is better able to employ interventions that maximize these benefits.

It is a vast oversimplification to speak about groups as if they were all alike. The literature is replete with comparisons of one kind of group to another (Brown, 1991; Garland, 1985; Papell & Rothman, 1962; Toseland & Rivas, 2001), and Chapter 4 will focus on various group typologies. At this point, the differences in group approaches can be summarized by pointing out that groups can focus primarily on interpersonal processes, on each individual's intrapsychic dynamics within the context of the group, or on the achievement of a common group goal, as in the task-oriented group. Group workers may assume an active or passive stance, create varying degrees and kinds of group structures, and may use activities or dialogue as the primary means of expression and communication. Groups may shift in any of these dimensions as member needs and circumstances change.

Whatever the group model or purpose, the understanding and recognition of the benefits it can provide serve as a guide for assessment and intervention. Yalom (1985) refers to these as "therapeutic factors," rather than "curative factors," in the recognition that professionals help people grow and change, but not necessarily to become cured. This book goes beyond consideration of therapeutically oriented groups to also consider the benefits of those designed to complete a task. It also identifies benefits that are defined by the value base of the social work profession.

The contributions of any group to its members will vary in nature and intensity with group purpose and model. Therefore, the following discussion of beneficial factors and implications should be considered within the framework of each particular group.

Beneficial Factors and Implications for Practice

Feeling Normal

Many people live with guilt or shame about their problems, believing or feeling that they are the only ones who have extremely mismanaged their lives or who have had to deal with a situation such as theirs. Being in a group with others who share their problems means that for at least the duration of each week's group meeting, people who feel their lives are abnormal can feel quite literally "normal." Feeling like one is not abnormal does not necessarily mean being healthy, but it does reduce the inhibitions that interfere with the ability to face a problem and to work towards its solution.

The implication of this factor for student practice is to show the importance of reinforcing the "we are all in the same boat" phenomenon. His/her opening remarks at the first meeting should focus on the fact that the members are all there because of the problem they share, and their desire to constructively deal with it. The very act of openly identifying the problem at the outset makes the unspeakable speakable, and helps the members do the work they need to do.

Opportunity to Hide

While many people might naturally assume that an introverted or shy individual would adapt more quickly to casework than group work intervention, it could also be argued that the opposite is true. Group members may fall anywhere on the introvert–extrovert continuum and such personality differences, often culturally influenced, potentially enhance the group experience. Paradise and Daniels (1976) define a properly balanced group as "one in which tensions and differences exist so that movement and action may take place.An unbalanced group is one in which all members are predominantly the same" (p. 41).

Reserved, cautious members can test the safety of the group experience by observing more outspoken, risk-taking members. Each exchange between the worker and one group member sends messages to all other members about how the worker will react to them and on their behalf. In a one-to-one situation the client can't rely on anyone else to test the situation, and this could be inhibiting to an introverted personality.

Students must be helped to appreciate this dynamic, and not pressure members to speak up if they wish to begin more as observing participants than active ones, especially during what Garland, Jones, and Kolodny (1976) refer to as "pre-affiliation," the first stage of group development. It is helpful to gently invite members to speak, as long as the student respects the varying needs for distance and privacy that members bring with them. In appreciation of this dynamic, the student should also be helped to resist the temptation to probe for deep underlying feelings early in the group's life. Superficiality is not artificiality. In fact, we often worry about people who cannot be superficial, and who spill out their deepest concerns indiscriminately. Students must learn to appreciate the normal human defenses members bring with them and to proceed accordingly.

Evoking New and Different Aspects of One's Personality

We all know that we behave somewhat differently with the various people in our lives. Some of our friends or family members are easy to talk with seriously and others may bring out our sense of humor. A person may have several personality facets evoked in a relationship with any one person, but even more emerge in a group situation with many people. Over time, the multiple relationships and interpersonal transactions within the group permit many aspects of a single member's personality structure to be revealed, including ones unexpressed prior to the group experience. Once expressed, these facets become accessible to interventions by the worker and other members.

Students must be helped to recognize the interchanges between members that bring out the most constructive behaviors and to reinforce these as they emerge. As members learn the value of honest communication, students may find themselves supporting responses that members may have formerly considered "impolite." Constructive behavior is not always pleasant, and a member's new found ability to be assertive and confrontational may be among the personality aspects to be supported.

Creating New Behavioral Norms

With success, group members can be socialized into new standards for interpersonal relationships and problem-solving processes. It is quite common for mental health professionals to overlook this path to behavioral change, as they focus on the psychological aspects of clients' problems. Within the group as a social microcosm, the worker helps members to create new behavioral norms. Norms developed through peer interaction have a greater impact on individuals and are more readily internalized than those passed down through the efforts of a single authority figure (Moore, 1971).

In order to use this dynamic to full advantage, students must help members to articulate group and individual goals in clearly stated behavioral outcomes. For example, if a group of volatile adolescents has agreed to the shared goal of nonviolent management of conflict, worker interventions that enforce this will come to be supported by other group members who have committed themselves to the establishment of this as a behavioral norm.

Imitating Behavior

Related to the socialization or acculturation factor is the recognition of the human tendency to imitate behavior, with or without awareness of so doing. Parents recognize that behavior is contagious in their concern about whom their children choose as friends. This fear of the "rotten apple" can be converted into a positive force influencing behavioral change.

Yalom (1985) states "In groups the imitative process is. . . diffuse, as patients may model themselves upon aspects of the other group members as well as of the worker" (p. 18). Members will often try on behaviors they witness within the group context. Yalom refers to social psychology research suggesting that therapists may underestimate the importance of this dynamic.

It is this dynamic that also heightens the value of the worker as a role model. As the worker models the acceptance of all members, as well as other positive interpersonal behaviors and ways of communicating, members may identify with him/her and adopt these behaviors as their own. We need not rely on internal self-awareness as a route to behavioral change. The student can be helped to realize that his/her own conduct in the group can, in and of itself, contribute to the growth of its members.

Growth through Giving

Erickson defines the seventh stage of human development as a conflict between Generativity and Stagnation (1963). He states that fulfillment and continuation of one's own personal growth is achieved through the process of contributing to others. Although Erickson refers especially to the passing on of knowledge to the next generation, his conceptualization of growing through giving is applicable to social group work. It is congruent with Yalom's (1985) identification of altruism as a therapeutic factor in group therapy. A member's own growth is promoted when he/she has the opportunity to not only be the recipient of services, but to give to others as well.

The student should be helped to guide member interactions into patterns that are mutually supportive. In their discussion of mutual aid groups, Gitterman and Shulman (1994) say,

> This is a helping system in which the clients need each other as well as the worker. This need to use each other, to create not one but many helping relationships, is a vital ingredient of the group process and constitutes a common need over and above the specific tasks for which the group was formed. (p. 14)

Interestingly, most professionals exclude themselves from this reciprocal process. Workers may become so concerned about being the giver that they sometimes overlook how empowering it is to the member who is able to give something back to them. A social work student once told of her feelings of discomfort when the adolescents in her charge focused their attention on her after she fell ill while on duty as a direct care worker in a residential setting. They insisted on bringing her tea and doing whatever else they could to help her feel more comfortable. The student recognized the wholesomeness of their motivation, and permitted them to care for her in this way. Nevertheless, she felt guilty and somehow thought she was "cheating" by being the recipient of their concern. She was helped to recognize that her behavior offered positive reinforcement to their nurturing impulses, as well as empowering them with a sense of competence. Students must be helped to recognize the multidirectional flow of give and take.

All of Us Are Smarter than Any One of Us

In his discussion of the advantages of group supervision, Kadushin (1992) describes the potential for several individuals working together to achieve greater success in solving a problem than individuals working alone on the same issue. The different perspectives and thoughts each person brings results in a synergism that is also an important dimension of social group work.

Almost any seasoned group worker or classroom teacher will be able to tell of instances in which the results of joint problem-solving efforts were superior to the advice or answer that the worker or teacher was prepared to offer. While at times, giving advice can be helpful and appropriate, the student must learn to help members engage in problem-solving processes through which members of a group may prove smarter than any single person, including the worker.

Reliving Early Family Life

Many group work theorists address the phenomenon of the group taking on the characteristics of a family. Garland et al. (1976) identify Stage III of group development as intimacy and say "As the character of group life becomes increasingly intimate, there are indications that the frame of reference for the experience becomes a familial one" (p. 50). As these transferences occur, members view each other as siblings and the worker as a parent figure. It is common to find references to formed groups as families outside of the professional literature as well. Decades ago the world learned about the infamous Manson family, and today neighborhood gangs are often referred to as "families."

Yalom (1985) identifies this phenomenon as a major therapeutic factor in the use of groups for therapeutic purposes. These dynamics provide opportunities for re-parenting, a factor that is especially important for group members with histories of early childhood parental neglect or abuse. The student must be helped to understand that the elements of good parenting in their simplest form—communicating caring and total acceptance of each member—will encourage a healing process. The safe, nonretaliatory environment set up by the worker is in itself an important part of group work practice.

Development of Social Skills

One must have at least basic social skills in order to become and remain a member of a group. Many of those we serve in groups are underdeveloped in this area. Whether it is the stated purpose of the group or a by-product of its processes, members can be helped to acquire or improve their interpersonal skills as a result of their group experience. Social isolation is in and of itself a contributing factor to antisocial and self-destructive behaviors. It is a valuable contribution to the lives of group members to help them gain the confidence and ability to develop a satisfying social existence.

Students are sure to have many instances in which a group member will engage in behaviors that turn people away. As such individuals are helped to understand the impact of their behavior on others, in an accepting nonjudgmental manner, they may be helped to correct the skewed perceptions of reality that can trigger antisocial responses and become freer to develop more socially acceptable behaviors.

For example, Schiller (1995) describes a group situation in which a very quiet group member, Lisa, began to address her discomfort speaking in the group. The worker knew that other members were becoming resentful of Lisa's noncommunicative behavior. The worker used this opportunity to ask Lisa if she would like feedback from the others about how they experienced her quietness. Lisa agreed. To her surprise, she learned that the others believed she was judging them and feeling above them. It had never occurred to her that her shyness and reticence could be interpreted as an insult to others. This incident was a turning point for her, and she began to participate more freely and frequently.

Students can be helped to encourage similar interpersonal learning in their groups by helping members understand the impact their behavior has on others.

Appreciating Diversity

The goal of social group work is to help group members comfortably live with differences. Social group work does not seek to promote conformity. It is a method based on democratic principles that apply to therapeutic as well as social action purposes. To this end, group development theory and research (Garland, et al., 1976; Sullivan, 1995), stress the importance of workers permitting rebellious actions that are not hurtful to others. The worker's nonretaliatory responses to challenges to his/her authority encourages honest expression of feelings and an openness to new perspectives, all of which promote creativity in problem-solving and in a general approach to life.

The respect for differences extends to acceptance of people from different races, ethnicities, and genders. There is much evidence that the group becomes a social microcosm of society at large, with the same status and power relationships developing within its boundaries (Brown & Mistry, 1994; Garvin & Reed, 1983; Shapiro, 1990). It is the worker's responsibility to consciously and actively work to counteract this potentially harmful dynamic. In certain instances it can be dealt with through careful consideration of group composition during the group formation process, (See Chapter 7 for further discussion of group composition issues) such as homogeneity in groups that have as their central task racial, ethnic, or gender identity. Groups may also have as their goal the bringing together of specific peoples, such as Arabic and Jewish people (Bargal & Bar, 1994), black and white people (Drower, 1993), or men and women (Garvin & Reed, 1983). Group composition issues are more clearly defined in these situations. Groups that focus on shared issues that transcend any one race or ethnicity, such as support groups for an illness, or groups to help members overcome childhood abuse, are frequently composed of racially and ethnically mixed members.

The student must be helped to first examine his/her own attitudes and possible stereotypic thinking, and to become vigilant in recognizing when potentially lower status members need support. Members must be helped to treat each other with equal respect and dignity. This challenge is among the more complex of those we face, but an awareness of the issue is at least a point at which to begin.

Getting the Job Done

Although the greatest emphasis in the practice and study of social group work is on groups which have as their major purpose the personal growth of group members, the method also includes work with task-oriented groups. These have as their purpose the attainment of a goal outside of the group and the personal growth of group members. Related to the concept that all of us are smarter than any one of us is the notion that all of us can achieve more than any one of us. According to Erickson (1963), the development of the desire to collaborate with others is a part of normal and healthy human growth. He defines latency, his fourth age of man, as "Industry versus Inferiority," and considers this "socially a most decisive stage: since industry involves doing things beside and with others, a first sense of division of labor and of differential opportunity" (p. 260). Though the major purpose of a group may be the completion of a task, the personal growth of members is often a byproduct of a successful group effort.

Professionals may assume that work with a task-oriented group such as a committee of staff or community members requires less skill than work with a treatment or personal growth group. This is not the case. Socio-emotive factors amongst group members, such as how the members feel about one another, can influence the alliances that develop and the way the group works as strongly as the considerations of the objective task-related realities.

Students must be helped to appreciate the value of task-oriented groups, and to apply all their knowledge of group dynamics in their work with them. The literature (Ephross & Vassil, 1988; Toseland & Rivas, 2001) identifies the practice issues which must be addressed in this work. These include values and ethics, contracting, group composition, group development, decision making, and conflict management. These are among the generic components of social group work that need to be considered in the task-oriented group as well as in any other.

Empowerment

The reason that many social work students and even some seasoned professionals feel anxiety about working with groups is the very reason to use them. Groups can be powerful, and individuals can be empowered through their membership in them. Concern about the power of the group may be one of the reasons for the widespread practice of professional co-leadership.

Empowerment practice can be conceptualized as helping clients, especially those from disempowered populations, to gain power and feel in control of their own lives (Fatout, 1995; Hegar & Hunzeker, 1988; Sue, 1981). It can also be conceptualized as helping clients engage in a political process to bring about societal change (Breton, 1994; Russell-Erlich & Rivera, 1986; Swift, 1984). Thought of in these ways, empowerment emerges as a goal of both personal growth and task-oriented groups. As members reap the benefits described earlier in this chapter, they become more able to advocate in their personal and political lives for their own well-being and that of their loved ones.

Students must be helped to recognize the elements that promote empowerment. These include awareness of one's inner and social self and of the environmental context of the group or the broader community or society. It includes recognizing oneself and being recognized as competent (Breton, 1994), being able to engage in productive decision-making processes (Ramey, 1993), and feeling strong enough to assert oneself in situations that challenge one's beliefs and perspectives. As students gain appreciation of these elements they will be better able to offer interventions that promote them.

Conclusion

An analysis and understanding of the factors in group life that help its members reach their goals, will lead to interventions that capitalize upon them. This chapter has identified many of these factors which can be used as a foundation for social group work practice.

References

Bargal, D., & Bar, H. (1994). The encounter of social selves: Intergroup workshops for Arab and Jewish youth. *Social Work with Groups, 17*(3), 39-60.

Breton, M. (1994). On the meaning of empowerment and empowerment-oriented social work practice. *Social Work with Groups, 17*(3), 23-38.

Brown, A., & Mistry, T. (1994). Group work with mixed membership groups: Issues of race and gender. *Social Work with Groups, 17*(3), 5-22.

Brown, L. N. (1991). *Groups for growth and change.* White Plains, NY: Longman.

Drower, S. (1993). The contribution of group work in a changing South Africa. *Social Work with Groups, 16*(3), 5-22.

Ephross, P., & Vassil, T. (1988). *Groups that work: Structure and process.* New York: Columbia University Press.

Erickson, E. H. (1963). *Childhood and society* (2nd ed.). New York: W. W. Norton.

Fatout, M. (1995). Using limits and structures for empowerment of children in groups. *Social Work with Groups, 17*(4), 55-70.

Garland, J. (1985). The relationship between social group work and group therapy: Can a group therapist be a social group worker too? In M. Parnes (Ed.), *Innovations in social group work: Feedback from practice to theory: proceedings of the Annual Group Work Symposium* (pp. 17-28). Binghamton, NY: Haworth.

Garland, J., Jones, H., & Kolodny, R. (1976). A model for stages of development in social work groups. In S. Bernstein (ed.), *Explorations in group work: Essays in theory and practice* (pp. 17-71). Boston: Charles River Books.

Garvin, C. D., & Reed, B. G. (1983). Gender issues in social group work: An overview. *Social Work with Groups, 6*(3/4), 5-18.

Gitterman, A., & Shulman, L. (1994). *Mutual aid groups, vulnerable populations, and the life cycle.* New York: Columbia University Press.

Hegar, R. L., & Hunzeker, J. M. (1988). Moving toward empowerment-based practice in public child welfare. *Social Work, 33*, 499-502.

Kadushin, A. (1992). *Supervision in social work.* New York: Columbia University Press.

Moore, S. (1971). Group supervision: Forerunner or trend reflector: Part II advantages and disadvantages. *Social Worker, 39*, 3-7.

Papell, C., & Rothman, B. (1962). Social group work models-possession and heritage. *Journal of Education for Social Work, 2*, 66-77.

Paradise, R., & Daniels, R. (1976). Group composition as a treatment tool with children. In S. Bernstein (Ed.), *Further exploration in group work* (pp. 34-54). Boston: Charles River Books.

Ramey, J. (1993). Group empowerment through learning formal decision making processes. *Social Work with Groups, 16*(1/2), 171-186.

Russell-Erlich, J. L., & Rivera, F. O. (1986). Community empowerment as a non-problem. *Journal of Sociology and Social Welfare, 13*, 451-465.

Schiller, L. Y. (1995). Stages of development in women's groups: A relational model. In R. Kurland & R. Salmon (Eds.), *Group work practice in a troubled society* (pp. 117-138). Binghamton, NY: Haworth.

Shapiro, B. Z. (1990). The social work group as a social microcosm: Frames of reference revisited. *Social Work with Groups, 13*(2), 5-21.

Sue, D. W. (1981). *Counseling the culturally different: Theory and practice*. New York: Wiley.

Sullivan, N. (1995). Who owns the group? The role of worker control in the development of a group: A qualitative research study of practice. *Social Work with Groups, 18*(2/3), 15-32.

Swift, C. (1984). Empowerment: An antidote for folly. *Prevention in Human Services, 3*, xi-xv.

Toseland, R. W., & Rivas, R. F. (2001). *An introduction to group work practice* (4th ed.). Neeedham Heights, MA: Allyn & Bacon.

Yalom, I. D. (1985). *The theory and practice of group psychotherapy* (3rd ed.). New York: Basic Books.

Chapter 3 | Preparations for Arranging and Supervising a Group Work Assignment

Most of us remember our first week of field work. Many of us alternated between wanting to jump right in, and to hide in a corner. Students continue to experience these competing impulses when encountering new situations, and even seasoned practitioners and field instructors find themselves feeling this way on occasion. In fact, developing and supervising group work assignments may be one of those occasions that bring out the "jumper" and "hider" in us. While there are no magic remedies for these feelings, the model of assessment presented in this chapter can help one avoid the consequences of jumping or hiding when it comes to group work assignments.

Following a discussion of common challenges in developing group work assignments, this chapter will guide field instructors through assessment of their own strengths and limitations, the agency as the environmental context for groups, and the identification of opportunities for group assignments. Included in the appendix at the end of this chapter is the worksheet summarizing the assessment model presented here. Suggestions for further reading on this subject include articles by Cohen (1995), Garland (1992), and Gitterman (1986).

Challenges to Agency Assessment

As Bertha Reynolds pointed out, "Practice is always shaped by the needs of the times, the problems they present, the fears they generate, the solutions that appeal, and the knowledge and skill available." (as cited in Ehrenright, 1985, p. 13). As a major component of social work practice, the assessment process is strongly influenced by the practitioner and agency environment.

While the vast majority of social workers are committed to the importance of a full process of assessment, we may find ourselves foreshortening assessment and planning, relying instead on "automatic" decision making. One symptom of automatic thinking is when assessments of all clients end in the same diagnosis or statement of needs. A second sign is when all treatment plans or intervention strategies are the same, focusing on either a single practice method (such as individual, family, group, or community work) or one practice model (such as behavioral, psychoanalytic, or social action interventions). A third sign of automatic decision making is when all clients are assessed as only needing services that the agency currently provides within its mission and area of expertise.

These signs of automatic thinking are sometimes evident in developing field work assignments. First, all students may be considered to have the same learning needs. Second, all students may be assigned the same activities, carried out in the same way. Finally, all student assignments may be limited to those activities that the agency comfortably feels are appropriate for social work interns.

Actual practice examples are often more subtle than those presented here, but they are symptomatic of a foreshortened assessment process that does little justice to clients or students. The "Aunt Fanny description" coined by Kadushin (1963), is often employed in agency assessments. Aunt Fanny descriptions contain elements of truth, but they are so vague and nonjudgmental that they could describe any agency environment (or, anyone's aunt). Such assessments provide an illusion of inquiry, but do little to help the student plan an effective group assignment.

While social agencies have been increasingly calling for group work services to effectively meet clients' needs (Edwards, 1990), closer assessment of the agency environment may identify obstacles that will need to be overcome in planning group assignments. In some agencies, field instructors may find it relatively easy to develop educationally sound group assignments. In other agencies, the process of assessment for group assignments may uncover evidence of "automatic" thinking or other barriers. Most troubling, automatic decision making can often go unnoticed and unchallenged, since it is culturally syntonic. It arises as an attempt to operate successfully within the agency system. Worker stress (McCann & Perlman, 1980), goal displacement (Perrow, 1986), and organizational changes (Brager & Holloway, 1992) are forces that lead to more automatic decision making, and social workers must continuously examine their own practice and supervision for its occurrence. However, a great deal of agency-based activity is founded on custom, tempered by professional judgment. It is often difficult to distinguish dangerous automatic thinking from an informed understanding of agency function and operation.

The assessment framework presented in the following pages provides a way to expose automatic thinking and realistically engage in planning group work assignments. At minimum, the assessment and planning process will result in a new level of understanding of agency function along with the establishment of group assignments for students.

Framework of Assessment for Group Work Assignments

This section is devoted to a three-phase assessment model to help understand the educational environment for group assignments. It begins with field instructors' self-assessment of feelings and knowledge about supervising students' social work practice with groups. Following this inventory, the model proceeds with an examination of the agency's past and present experience with groups. It concludes with an analysis of client needs, agency capacities, and further planning strategies to establish group work assignments.

Phase One: Self-assessment

Field instructors themselves are not divorced from the agency environment. They are part of the system, and can embody strengths and weaknesses of the system. Field instructors' practice skills may be concentrated in one area, often contributing to reticence in creating assignments in other areas. Well-intentioned responses to demands to develop group assignments can be compromised by insufficient capacity to design, supervise, and evaluate group work assignments. Therefore, beginning the agency assessment process with an inward look is important to evaluate one's readiness to undertake the challenge of group assignments. Field instructors may begin this process by asking themselves the following focusing questions.

How do I feel about planning and supervising group work assignments?

Answers to the first question will help field instructors to identify their own concerns and biases before approaching work with students. It parallels the "tuning-in" (Schwartz, 1971) process that a worker engages in before approaching work with clients. This process raises a worker's consciousness before engagement, cueing the worker to potential pitfalls with enough time to lessen their impact on practice (Shulman, 1999).

Field instructors may need to cultivate their skills in perception to engage in this type of assessment. The following four related skills (Middleman & Wood, 1990) are particularly valuable in approaching a system of great familiarity (such as one's own professional self). First, "looking with planned emptiness" suggests that field instructors deliberately reserve an area in their mind for new discoveries. This will help to encourage openness to new observations rather than rationalizing or avoiding them. Second, "looking at the old as if new," incorporates elements of playfulness in taking a look at oneself and familiar agency activities and structure. Third, "jigsaw puzzling" reminds field instructors that although they can know most of the pieces of their personal "puzzle," they may be missing a critical part, or they may need to rearrange the pieces to see them fit together. The fourth skill of perception, "looking from diverse angles," is particularly well suited to field instruction. In taking on the role of educator, field instructors have already begun to see their professional work in new ways. By diversifying the angles from which they assess their own feelings and capabilities, students and instructors expand their opportunities for understanding.

Perhaps the most difficult charge in assessment is trying to separate the expected outcome of the assessment from the process itself. The often-quoted statement: "if all you have is a hammer, all you see is a nail" is appropriate in this discussion. We must make sure that our assessments do not become self-fulfilling prophecies in which our own frame of reference and anticipated outcomes determine our findings.

What experience and knowledge about groups can I bring to this process?

Once field instructors can identify and deal with their own feelings about group assignments, they are ready to reach for the information to help them succeed. This second question directs field instructors to look for their own group social work skills and knowledge. This inquiry may lead to a reconnection with group work knowledge, suggest gaps that can be filled, or both.

For some time now, most graduate schools have incorporated social work with groups in an "integrated," "clinical," or "generalist" curriculum, with only nine schools offering a two-year concentration in group work. (Birnbaum, 1990; Birnbaum & Auerbach, 1994). Although social work with groups can be taught effectively with a multilevel approach, recent studies show that group work is not integrated to the extent necessary in many schools of social work (Birnbaum &

Wayne, 2000). In their 1989 study of sources of practitioners' knowledge in group work, Birnbaum, Middleman, and Huber found group work knowledge came from many sources, yet few respondents credited their formal graduate education. Field instructors may find that their experience is similar, and may have gained knowledge and experience with groups from other arenas.

What experience and knowledge about generalist practice can I draw on?

The third question helps field instructors examine their broad base of social work experience and knowledge for elements that can be brought into service in supervising group assignments. Successful field instruction of group assignments results from mixing specific group work knowledge with a professional foundation in social work practice and an understanding of the dynamics of field education (Cohen, 1993). Principles of generalist social work practice suggest that key skills such as engagement, developing goals, contracting, and evaluation are applicable to all sizes of client systems. Thus, one can draw on this knowledge base as one conducts an assessment to develop new groups, as well as once the groups are underway.

The social work group can be seen as a client system that goes through a series of stages, dealing with similar concerns as all systems, including dynamic equilibrium, boundary maintenance, negative entropy, and equifinality (Germain, 1975). The identification of the group itself as a distinct entity, or "second client" (Shulman, 1999), sets the stage to draw on both generic and specific practice principles for social work with groups. Simply listening to workers describe a group's "personality" or "defenses," suggests that a knowledge of working with individual clients is often applicable to work with groups.

Further, the ecosystems perspective and life model of social work practice direct practitioners to look at the system(s) in which clients operate in order to understand the reciprocal relationships among clients, other people, and environments (Germain & Gitterman, 1996). Field instructors can draw on this knowledge, as it applies to work with smaller and larger systems (such as communities, agencies, and organizations) to assist them in supervising students' group assignments.

What do I need to do to prepare myself to plan and supervise group work assignments?

The final question in this phase of the assessment asks field instructors to identify learning needs and a plan to meet them. Plans should include accessing knowledge from work in other areas of practice and supervision that can be brought into service with group assignments. Self development plans can include specialized training in social group work practice, consultation with agency colleagues, and review of current literature. The final chapter of this book provides suggestions on further learning opportunities in social work with groups.

It is helpful to remember that all social workers have some gaps in knowledge and needs for professional renewal. It is not suggested that all gaps must be filled before approaching students. We provide the best possible role model to student interns when we practice self-evaluation, identifying and enhancing our own skills in a thoughtful, developmental manner.

Phase Two: Identifying Past and Present Agency Experience

The field instructor must identify and understand the agency's history, formal and informal policies, expertise, and beliefs about social work practice with groups and group work assignments for students. This analysis of the agency context includes: "conditions existing in the agency or host setting that may have an impact on worker action and on the group that is being formed" (Kurland, Getzel, & Salmon, 1986, p. 61). As in the first phase of the assessment, questions that raise awareness are helpful in launching the examination of the agency environment. The following questions (adapted from Karp, undated), focus on the agency's ideology, history, and norms, providing the second stage for this inquiry.

Is there an agency ideology on group methods?

The identification and understanding of agency ideology is critical in developing a strategy of integration for group work assignments. Group work assignments can operate outside of the mainstream of agency activity, but students' learning and client service may be compromised if this path is taken without thorough assessment of possible implications.

It may seem difficult at first to speculate on an agency's ideology about groups. However, field instructors can reflect on what they have heard or read at the agency on the subject of groups and group work. For example, statements like "Groups don't work here!" or "We believe in groups for everyone!" recall the examples of automatic thinking discussed earlier in this chapter. When repeated often enough, these comments take on the power of myth, framing the agency's ideology. Students' assignments will operate under this belief system.

What has been the agency experience with groups?

The agency's ideology is closely linked to its history with groups in general and students' group assignments in particular. The agency's translation of its history has a strong bearing on group development and progress. In agencies without a broad use of group methods, this history may have been written long ago, by a small number of practitioners. This history can be found through formal documents as well as informal discussions with agency "sages" who can retell stories from the past. It is critical to understand the present interpretation of past activities and how they may affect future initiatives. Regardless of the clients who participated, the purpose of the groups, or the skills of the workers, this past experience exerts great influence on an agency's current receptivity to groups.

Of course, it is possible to benefit from the successful past history of work with groups, but sadly, negative recollections are common. When agency administrators and workers report past failures with groups, field instructors and students should be on notice that a good deal of political negotiation will be needed to launch a group assignment.

Do certain groups of staff have a monopoly on working with groups?

Agencies often delegate areas of work to particular groups of agency staff. When a small cadre appears to have a monopoly on work with groups, it will be important to identify their professional orientation and any common operating principles. In multidisciplinary settings, ownership of groups may not be held by social workers, but by teachers, psychologists, or nurses. These professions have developed extensive knowledge and skills in working with groups and often control the assignment of leaders. It may first appear that a social group work assignment is impossible in such a setting. However, the knowledge gained during assessment can be used in efforts to modify or change agency policy.

Similarly problematic, students may be initially offered only opportunities to co-lead with an experienced group facilitator. Field instructors should consider this option carefully, since different professions have significantly different views on the purposes and processes of groups. Further, co-leadership with any experienced professional (including social workers) often turns out to be assisting or watching. Field instructors may make the common mistake of thinking that students are working with a group when they are merely observers. Learning from role models can be valuable, but apprenticeship learning is no substitute for independent group leadership in learning social work with groups (Wayne & Garland, 1990).

If no agency staff work with groups, what can be the reason(s)?

The assessment process may indicate that groups are seen as too specialized or difficult for student interns in some agencies. In others it may be felt that group work opportunities are too precious to share or not worthy of professional effort. Students' group assignments can forge new areas of service delivery, but it would be advisable to first look for group assignments that complement, rather than compete with, existing group activities. As already noted, such efforts, if successful, will ease interprofessional or interdepartmental tensions and enhance the group's chance of success.

The choice of what services to provide, who should provide them, and how they should be provided should be interpreted as purposive agency decisions. Gitterman and Miller (1989) point out: "Almost all, if not all clinical decisions represent agency policy and organizational imperatives in action" (p. 32). Making these choices visible, understandable, and open to interpretation and change are key tasks in agency assessment.

Phase Three: Client Needs and Agency Capacities

The focusing questions in this stage of the agency assessment should be asked by both field instructors and students once they have reached a comfortable level of understanding an agency's history and current state of receptivity towards groups. Among the following questions, the first broadens the inquiry, the second brings the assessment back to agency realities, and the third sets the stage for launching the assignment.

Are there unmet client and staff needs in this agency which can be appropriately met through the use of social group work methods?

Answering the first question in this phase of work can liberate field instructor and student from the present and past operations of the agency, and encourage them to look at one of the most important determinants in developing assignments, client needs. One of the benefits of engaging in a broad assessment is a deeper understanding of agency mission, goals, and service delivery strategies. This understanding can, in turn, inspire expansive thinking. This stage of assessment may result in innovative services to meet client needs through groups.

The process can highlight the way agencies define their client base, their needs, and the ways in which some needs are met. The analysis challenges field instructors and students to address unmet needs in new ways.

Student assignments are often developed in haste, simply to meet a school requirement. However group assignments, like all other student assignments, should be judged on the basis of potential effectiveness in meeting the needs of clients. Successful groups are "critical" (Cohen, 1995) in that they address significant needs as articulated by clients and others. Students should be encouraged to ask if there are clients who could benefit from groups in any of the 12 ways described in chapter 2.

In addition to suggesting new service areas for clients, the assessment can also provide an overview of agency operations and staff relationships, pointing to opportunities for group assignments with administrative groups and committees. This assessment process may suggest areas in which staff groups would be useful, such as in developing new programs and enhancing intra-agency collaboration. Students' group assignments should be planned and implemented to incorporate a collective purpose, the opportunity for democratic decision making, and some degree of member flexibility. Many staff groups can accommodate these basic requirements within existing authority structures.

In what ways will agency policies, procedures, and informal organization enhance or complicate the student's work with a group?

Although group assignments are critical in the education of social workers and can be of significant help to clients, they must be presented and nurtured with an understanding of formal and informal agency structures (Gitterman, 1986). The failure to consider synchronization of the goals and methodology of the group assignment with the mission and function of the agency setting often places group programs outside the real work of the agency (Garland, 1992). When groups are seen as "frills" (Kurland, Getzel, & Salmon, 1986), they are often the first assignments to be sacrificed when other priorities emerge.

Groups that are not integrated into the agency environment can be marginalized, receiving little support and supervisory attention. Even the most basic arrangements, such as rooms and a budget for refreshments should be considered in light of how they would impact the potential group assignment. Further examples, such as intake procedures and documentation requirements will affect the group, and unless known, may sabotage students' efforts. Simple considerations, such as whether the room selected for a children's group is next door to a worker who requires quiet, are often overlooked. As case studies demonstrate, exploring and establishing a good fit for groups and group work assignments in the agency context is crucial (Cohen, 1995).

How will the student and field instructor proceed to develop and implement the group assignment?

Although it would be a relief to know that with this question, the process of assessment is over and real work can begin, that is clearly not the case. Rather, this question asks the student and field instructor to map out the next stages of their process of developing a group assignment. However, as the next planning phase begins, student and field instructor are far more knowledgeable and grounded in the agency environment, and are able to use their experience to suggest an effective purpose, composition, structure, and content for the group assignment.

When the assessment has revealed that social workers do not have a positive history or foothold with groups in the agency, the assignment planning effort will need to include agency-based advocacy. Field instructors and students may find themselves in the position of "policy entrepreneur" (Kingdon, 1984), selling the notion of group work assignments and their benefits for serving clients. In order to develop a persuasive case, the instructor and student must consider the data gathered during each stage of the assessment process and further analyze the reasons for the absence of groups. They must identify ways that this absence may be overtly or subtly encouraged through agency policies and practices. Before making their case to agency administrators and colleagues, the instructor and student should develop a strategy to deal with obstacles, capitalizing on ways that group assignments will benefit students, clients, and agency.

Conclusion

Once field instructors have a solid understanding of their own strengths and limitations, and a beginning understanding of the agency context for groups, they can engage in an assessment partnership with students. This model of partnership, rather than one of the expert and apprentice, enables students to participate in critical assessment and planning activities. Together, field instructor and student can assess the student's skills and interests, as well as agency receptivity to social work groups, and agency supports and barriers to group work assignments. Their partnership models group work practice in that field instructor and student, like group members, each make their unique contribution towards the accomplishment of a collective purpose.

When students participate in this process, they learn that neither jumping nor hiding are appropriate strategies for successful social work practice with groups. Too often, students and workers are directed to "Do a group!" (Garland, 1992), and given no chance to self-reflect and plan. This assessment model described here serves to hold back jumpers until they are ready. And, engaging in a planning partnership can bring out even the best hider, since group work assignments can be said to begin as soon as the student begins the assessment process. Most importantly, participating in pre-group development activities with field instructors insures that students do not neglect this important area of work, dramatically enhancing the quality of social work service to clients.

References

Birnbaum, M. (1990, June). *Group work, the spotted owl: An endangered species in social work education*. Paper presented at the 12th Annual Symposium on Social Work with Groups, Miami, FL.

Birnbaum, M., & Auerbach, C. (1994). Groupwork in graduate social work education: The price of neglect. *Journal of Social Work Education*, *30*, 325-335.

Birnbaum, M., Middleman, R., & Huber. R. (1989). *Where social workers obtain their knowledge base in group work*. Paper presented at the Annual Meeting of the National Association of Social Workers, San Francisco, CA.

Birnbaum, M., & Wayne, J. (2000). Group work content in foundation generalist education: The necessity for change. *Journal of Social Work Education*, *36*, 347-356.

Brager, G., & Holloway, S. (1992). Assessing prospects for organizational change: The uses of force field analysis. *Administration in Social Work*, *16*(3/4), 15-28.

Cohen, C. S. (1993). Enhancing social group work opportunities in field work education (Doctoral dissertation, Graduate School and University Center of the City University of New York, 1993). *Dissertation Abstracts International*, *29*(3), 970.

Cohen, C. S. (1995). Making it happen: Building successful support group programs. *Social Work with Groups*, *18*(1), 67-80.

Edwards, R. L. (1990). From the president: Creating a niche for social group work. *NASW News*, *35*(4), 2.

Ehrenright, J. (1985). *The altruistic imagination*. Ithaca, NY: Cornell University Press.

Garland, J. (1992). Developing and sustaining group work services: A systemic and systematic view. *Social Work with Groups, 15*(4), 89-98.

Germain, C. (1975). A theoretical view of the life model: Eco-systems Perspective. In Germain, Goldstein, & Maluccio. *Workshop on the ecological approach and clinical practice* (pp.1-25). West Hartford, CT: Connecticut Society for Clinical Social Work and University of Connecticut School of Social Work.

Germain, C., & Gitterman, A. (1996). *The life model of social work practice: Advances in theory and practice* (2nd ed.). New York: Columbia University Press.

Gitterman, A. (1986). Developing a new group service. In A. Gitterman & L. Shulman (Eds.), *Mutual aid groups and the life cycle* (pp.53-71). Itasca, IL: F.E. Peacock.

Gitterman, A., & Miller, I. (1989). The influence of the organization on clinical practice. *Clinical Social Work Journal, 17*(2), 151-164.

Kadushin, A. (1963). Diagnosis and evaluation for (almost) all occasions. *Social Work, 8*(1), 12-19.

Karp, I. (undated). *Strategy of entry*. New York: New York University School of Social Work.

Kingdon, J. W. (1984). *Agenda, alternatives and public policies*. Boston: Little Brown.

Kurland, R., Getzel, G., & Salmon, R. (1986). Sowing groups in infertile fields: Curriculum and other strategies to overcome resistance to the formation of new groups. In M. Parnes (Ed.), *Proceedings of the annual group work symposium. Innovations in social group work: Feedback from practice to theory* (pp.57-74). Binghamton, NY: Haworth.

McCann, L., & Perlman, L. A. (1990). Vicarious traumatization: A framework for understanding the psychological effects of working with victims. *Journal of Traumatic Stress, 3*(1), 131-146

Middleman, R. R., & Wood, G. G. (1990). *Skills for direct practice in social work*. New York: Columbia University Press.

Perrow, C. (1986). *Complex organizations* (3rd ed.). New York: Random House.

Schwartz, W. (1971). On the use of groups in social work practice. In W. Schwartz & S. R. Zalba (Eds.), *The practice of group work* (pp.3-24). New York: Columbia University Press.

Shulman, L. (1999). *The skills of helping individuals, families, groups and communities* (4th ed.). Itasca, IL: F.E. Peacock.

Wayne, J., & Garland, J. (1990). Groupwork education in the field: The state of the art. *Social Work with Groups, 13*(2), 95-109.

(Appendix begins on page 30)

Appendix

Worksheet: Guide to Preparation for Social Work with Groups

These focusing questions guide field instructors, social workers, and students through a process of identifying their readiness for working with groups, assessing the agency environment as the context for social work practice with groups, and understanding client needs in relation to agency capacities.

Phase One: Self-Assessment of Social Workers

A. How do I feel about planning, leading, and supervising social work groups?

B. What experience and knowledge about social work practice with groups can I bring to this process?

C. What experience and knowledge about social work practice in general can I draw on?

D. What do I need to do to prepare myself to plan and lead social work groups?

Phase Two: Identification of Past and Present Agency Experience with Groups

A. Is there an agency ideology on group methods?

B. What has been the agency experience with groups?

C. Do certain groups of staff have a monopoly on working with groups?

D. If agency staff does not work with groups, what can be the reason(s)?

Phase Three: Assessment of Client Needs and Agency Capacities

A. Are there unmet client and staff needs in this agency which can be appropriately met through the use of social work with groups?

B. In what ways will agency policies, procedures, and informal organization enhance or complicate the work of the group?

C: How will we proceed to develop and implement the group assignment?

Chapter 4 | Types and Models of Group Work Practice

Because of the overlapping purposes and elements in various group types, it is neither possible nor desirable to make a list of group work models that are presented as totally different from each other. For example, educational groups can provide support, and support groups have therapeutic effects (Garland, 1986). Wasserman and Danforth (1988), note that "A helping process that is not conceptualized as therapeutic may be just as therapeutic, if not more so, than one that is. This may be the case of support group vis-a-vis the therapy group (p. 66). According to Toseland and Rivas (2001), "therapy groups help members change their behavior, cope with or ameliorate their personal problems, or rehabilitate themselves after physical, psychological, or social trauma" (p. 26). Although these authors go on to point to the remedial and rehabilitative focus of therapy groups, each of the purposes they describe could be attributed to educational and support groups as well.

Given their overlapping elements, it is helpful to conceptualize groups as if they were viewed under a floodlight rather than a spotlight. A spotlight lights up an area with a clearly delineated boundary. There is nothing to see or consider in the surrounding darkness. A floodlight provides a major focus, but allows one to see it within the framework of the dimmer peripheral area. Students often err by mentally spotlighting a group type and losing sight of related though not central factors to be considered. They may also err in the other direction and lose sight of the major purpose. The resulting practice may be either too rigid or lacking in focus.

Following are four hypothetical situations presented by hypothetical students that represent the kinds of group situations actual students present to classroom and field instructors, and which contain elements of common dilemmas. An understanding of the range of group types and models and the similarities and differences among them would help actual students answer their own questions. The first situation is presented by a student we'll call Jeannie, who explains:

> I run a support group for elderly widows who have lost an adult child. At the last meeting, one of the women suggested that the group celebrate birthdays with cake and coffee. The members seem to like the idea, but I feel uncomfortable. They can go to the community center for their social lives. I'm supposed to be helping them grieve their losses, not joining them in birthday parties. What is the best way to explain this to them?

Tom presents the following problem:

> I'm placed in a junior high school and run a parenting skills group for parents of acting-out teen-teenagers. My co-leader and I don't think the parents are really motivated to learn new ways to handle their children. They come regularly, but never read the articles we give them. They seem to want to spend their time together trading family war stories. How can we keep them focused on the material we need to cover? The articles could really help them.

Francine talks about working with a holiday party planning committee of an association for diabetics. The committee members are themselves diabetic, and Francine says:

> They have begun to use committee meetings to discuss the stresses and anxieties of their disease. It's so good to see them use each other in this way that I hate to interrupt them even though they almost don't get to plan for the party, and we are behind schedule. I'm not sure what I should do.

Jim tells his frustrating story:

> The doctors in the hospital where I am placed have asked the social workers to help get the hypertension patients to take their medications in spite of their unpleasant side effects. My field instructor has assigned me to organize a support group in order for the patients to encourage each other to take better care of themselves. I just can't seem to get the group started. I've posted notices all over the hospital, sent letters to the prospective members and asked doctors and nurses to urge their patients to attend. Still, not one person showed up for the first meeting last Wednesday evening. These patients haven't asked to meet around their disease, but that's what I'm expected to get them to do. I don't know what to do next.

Each of these students is describing a dilemma in a different kind of social work group, each with its own purpose, and recognizes that their interventions must relate to the type of group their members have agreed or will agree to form. All groups should operate within a working agreement that sets the stage for member expectations and worker interventions.

Jeannie needs to recognize the celebration of birthdays as a constructive step towards healing the wounds of loss. Tom needs to listen to what the parents are saying to each other and to find the seeds of a curriculum that has more meaning to them than the articles he wishes they would read. Francine is in danger of overlooking the group's major purpose and needs to help the members work on their agreed upon task, planning the holiday party. She could offer the committee members a different group opportunity for mutual support around their illness. Jim needs to know that there are other group work options for the work he wishes to do besides trying to get members to attend a group meeting at a time he has chosen, to address a topic he believes is in their best interests to discuss.

Defining Group Types

When classroom teachers ask students to describe the kinds of groups they have been assigned in the field, their responses will usually reflect a wide range of ways to categorize groups. They might mention a support group for single mothers, a mandatory group for drunk drivers, a single session group for newly diagnosed cancer patients, or an after-school activity group for eight-year-olds. As in the examples given, group types can be described according to many different dimensions. These include group purpose (support), how the group was formed (mandatory), group structure (single session), or group content (activities). These dimensions overlap with each other, so that groups with the same purpose can differ in many ways. They may be long- or short-term, and have open-ended or closed membership. They may rely primarily on dialogue or include activities as a medium for expression, communication, and personal development.

In spite of all these possible variations, certain defining characteristics must be present in order for work with groups to be considered social work with groups. One of these is the worker's focus on helping members to meet each other's "human needs through democratic group processes" (Falk, 1995, p. 69). Social work with groups also requires the development of a common goal and purpose that integrates the personal goals of each member and the professional goals of the worker (Pappell & Rothman, 1980). The group worker is not the group leader, but instead seeks to promote members' autonomy and independence through support of positive indigenous leadership as it emerges through group development processes. These principles stem from the historical roots of this social work method that developed from a democratic movement. They must be present in all of the group types and formats discussed in this chapter, whether they are described by purpose, formation process, structure, or content.

Groups Defined by Purpose

Group work theorists categorize group purposes in many different ways. For example, Toseland and Rivas (1998) define groups as being either for treatment or task purposes. They consider treatment as the broad category in which all other personal growth groups fall. In contrast, this book considers personal growth, rather than treatment as an overarching category, largely because of its health and strengths perspective. Such an approach reflects the heritage of social group work, and its contribution to the social work profession.

Though students must be helped to understand the differences between groups that are designed for personal growth and those designed for task achievement, they must also recognize that to some extent, this is a false dichotomy. Growth groups may include tasks, and successful task achievement certainly promotes individual growth and development. Pappell and Rothman (1962), in their discussion of the social goals model (i.e., groups organized for affecting social change) refer to the underlying assumption that there is a unity between social action and individual psychological health. They point to the therapeutic and growth promoting implications of social participation. Nevertheless, as students consider the direction of their interventions, it remains helpful to distinguish between groups designed primarily for personal growth and those designed to complete a task.

Personal growth groups vary in their degree of emphasis on education, support, therapy/treatment and socialization. Task groups include agency or community committees, boards of directors, staff meetings, and other work groups.

Educational Groups

The purpose of social work educational groups is to help members gain new knowledge that will influence their psychosocial functioning. These groups are characterized as having a specific focus and addressing specific content areas, like Tom's group on parenting skills. They are generally time-limited, informative, and structured to facilitate the learning of new information, behaviors, and relationship skills (Kuechler, 1997). Other examples include groups on caretaking, learning to cope with and manage an illness, or overcoming an addiction.

There are important differences between an educational group that is part of social group work and other kinds of educational groups. The latter may focus primarily on providing new knowledge to members, while social work educational groups also attend to the psychosocial factors that influence how that information will be received, internalized, and put to use. Social work educational groups are called for when the nature of the new information brings questions, anxieties, and concerns that need to be addressed for the new knowledge to be useful and valuable. These groups require workers with both teaching and social group work skills. The student must help participants move beyond their roles as learners into the roles of group members engaged in mutual aid. Educational groups become social work groups "when the aim of...[the] activity is to assist clients to teach each other (Falk, 1995, p. 69).

Students may feel comforted and supported by going into a group with a prepared structure or curriculum, like Tom and his co-leader. However, they must be encouraged not to become so committed to *covering* material, that they overlook the importance of *uncovering* material. For example, a father in this group may quickly learn that the experts do not believe in corporal punishment as a response to an acting-out child. The student, however, must then recognize that although this father may readily give sincere verbal agreement to this notion, it will probably be difficult for him to implement the new approach when he is flooded with angry emotions evoked by his child's provocative behavior. A worker in Tom's situation must help the parents to deal with the challenges and potential conflicts the new information or new perspectives produce, and help them feel safe enough within the group to express feelings that they are not supposed to have. Tom's acceptance of these in a nonjudgmental manner can help the parents face and hopefully modify their feelings and inclinations towards less effective parental responses.

Any form of structure a student brings into the group must have a liberating rather than constricting effect on group processes. Structure can liberate by providing a focus, direction, and channel for the group's energy. However, in instances such as the one Tom and his co-leader faced, students must be prepared to let go of their curriculum structure as they receive direct or indirect cues about what the group members consider their most immediate concerns to be. Any form of social work must start where the client is, even if that place is not where the curriculum assumes they must be.

Support Groups

The purpose of support groups is to help members relieve stress and develop constructive behaviors to deal with difficult situations. They are not designed to cure mental illness or bring about overall personality change. Support groups are composed of people who share a similar set of challenging circumstances and who could help each other through an exchange of their experiences, ideas, and feelings (Wasserman & Danforth, 1988). Such circumstances could include dealing with loss, as was the issue in Jeannie's group, living with a chronic illness as in Jim's proposed group, or membership in a population suffering from discrimination because of ethnicity, race, physical disability, or sexual orientation. Members of support groups who demonstrate personality or emotional problems that severely limit the helpfulness of the support may need to be referred to a different kind of group.

On a cognitive–affective continuum, support groups are closer to the affective realm than educational groups. However, there is great overlap in these groups (Garland, 1986), and they are not distinctly different than each other. The best educational groups help members support each other as they learn. The best support groups will usually provide some information about the problem that members share and for which they seek to develop coping behaviors.

Socialization Groups

The purpose of socialization groups is to help members develop attitudes and behaviors that will help them contribute to and receive satisfaction from participation in daily community life. Such groups could be composed of children or youths being helped to develop age appropriate social competencies such as dealing with complex emotions, managing interpersonal conflict, and learning to share, create, and make decisions with others. The student who described her assignment as an after-school activity group may have been describing a group for these purposes.

Socialization groups can be helpful for any population that would benefit from a new view of their social selves. This includes isolated mothers who need to develop the necessary skills to become part of a supportive social network (Wayne, 1979), or elderly people who may be in need of resocialization into the changing social and family roles that come in later years (Hartford & Lawton, 1997).

Socialization groups usually seek to create group situations that mirror daily life events. Ordinary life experiences include recreational and work-oriented activities (see section on activity groups) and informal discussion of members' recent and past experiences, interests, pleasures, and problems. It is this broad purpose and use of content, as well as general informality that distinguishes this type of group from those that are focused on helping members improve a specific area of functioning. Its usual lack of a presenting problem further distinguishes this type of group work from most work with individuals.

Opportunities for socialization are omnipresent with natural groups in their daily living environment, whether in a residential or community setting. When possible, it may be more effective for the student to find rather than form such groups (see section on natural groups).

Therapy Groups

The purpose of a therapy group is to bring about personal changes in the behavior, cognition or affect of its members. Barker (1987) defines therapy as "a systematic process and activity designed to remedy, cure, or abate some disease, disability, or problem" (p. 164). Therapy groups focus on the personal problems of group members, as compared to support groups that focus on helping them to cope with the difficult circumstances they share. Despite the focus on individual personal problems, students must help members identify the connecting threads that create opportunities for members to be helpful to each other in some way.

There are as many types of therapy groups as there are theories of therapeutic approaches. As with one-to-one work, each of these theories has implications for the structure and focus of therapeutic interventions.

Task-oriented Groups

Task-oriented groups are those designed for the achievement of a goal outside of the group that affects a broader constituency than the group members themselves. Its "overriding purpose is to accomplish a goal that is neither intrinsically nor immediately linked to the needs of the members of the group" (Toseland & Rivas, 2001, p. 15). In task groups, assessments of individuals and group processes are made in relation to achievement of the group's task. Any resulting personal growth of members is viewed as a by-product of the group's major purpose.

Francine's holiday party planning committee was established as a task-oriented group. Hopefully, the working agreement articulated her responsibility to help the members plan a successful party. When they drifted into using the committee as a support group for personal issues, it would be Francine's job to help them remain focused on their task. It would not have been in their or anyone's interest to produce a poorly planned holiday party. Francine could create support group opportunities for the committee members at another point. They could agree to remain after committee meetings to resume their more personal discussions, or come together as a support group after the party had occurred.

Task-oriented groups frequently follow formalized rules for discussion and decision making. Members are chosen for their potential contribution as individuals or representatives to the task at hand. A student may assume a direct leadership role in such a group, or may serve as a staff person and consultant to a group chaired by a layperson. In these instances, the student can provide direct feedback to the group from his/her assigned role, or can confer with the chair outside of meetings, to help him/her keep the group directed towards its agreed upon purpose. In either case, it is the student as social group worker who brings knowledge and skill about group work practice to the group experience.

Although task-group membership does not entail sharing personal and intimate material, the socio-emotive factors of personal and interpersonal feelings amongst members still affect group processes. Whether for political, personal, or other reasons, subgroups and alliances develop, and these may have either a positive or negative effect on successful completion of the task.

The most common error students make in their work with task groups is to overlook these socio-emotive factors, and to proceed as if all that occurred in the group were based on objective thought, without the influence of personal feelings. Professional social workers sometimes overlook the fact that the same skilled professionalism required for work with personal growth groups is necessary for task groups as well. Ephross and Vassil (1988) assert that "a steadily increasing concern with gaining skills in group methods in treatment. . . has not been accompanied by corresponding attention to working groups" (p. 7). It is the ability to assess the group dynamics and to intervene purposefully, informed by knowledge of group work practice, and directed by the values of the profession that separates the social group worker from the lay chairperson, and which makes task groups a model of social group work practice.

Groups Defined by the Formation Process

All groups can be categorized as either natural or formed. Natural groups are those in which people come together either because of geographic proximity, shared interests or goals, shared circumstances, or family ties. Most students, however, are assigned to work with groups that are formed by professionals for a particular purpose. Formed groups may be composed of voluntary or mandated members.

Natural Groups

Natural groups refer to those that form without professional intervention. They exist in residential as well as community settings and are there to be found rather than formed by the professionals who wish to work with them (Frey, 1966). Natural groups offer special opportunities for social work practice. The level of communication and accessibility to feelings that workers try to foster in formed groups often occur spontaneously amongst people who have come together naturally, and who have been together for a period of time. Ironically, in both residential and community settings, it is often paraprofessional direct practice workers rather than professional social workers who have opportunities to intervene in such circumstances.

Work with natural groups is as challenging as with formed groups. The student should not assume that the existing relationships amongst group members are conflict-free or necessarily built on trust and affection. There are times when the student as the new member of the group may have to help members unlearn their less effective ways of relating and communicating with each other.

There are many opportunities for students in different settings to reach out to naturally grouped target populations. These include common living areas where people in residential settings spend their unstructured time, community center drop-in lounges, and high school cafeterias. In the community, natural groups can be found in playgrounds, on neighborhood street corners, shopping malls, and fastfood restaurants. Adolescents, who may be difficult to engage within an agency setting, may respond positively to the social work student who reaches out to them in such places (Bass, 1995).

Students may feel awkward reaching out to natural groups as the new and usually uninvited members. They must be as honest and clear about their purpose and function as they would be in a more traditional, formed group. This may be more difficult to do away from the security of an office and a presenting problem focus. This is not social work practice as usual, and requires a different perspective of professional self than in the more traditional therapeutic hour. Chapter 7 elaborates on how to help students develop skills for engaging groups in natural, unstructured situations.

Social group work has its roots in working with natural groups, and the profession's movement away from prevention and education has resulted in doing so less frequently than before. Students should be helped to recognize when this approach may be the most effective.

Formed Groups

Students will be assigned either to work with groups that have
already been formed by another professional, or like Jim be asked to
form a group themselves. Though students may sometimes not recognize it as such, forming a group is as much a part of group work practice as is the work done at any meeting. While chapter 7 will elaborate
on group formation skills, this section will describe the characteristics of formed groups.

Formed groups may be composed of members who are there by
choice or because they must attend in order to avoid some negative
consequence. The negative consequence could be an angry spouse, a
legal consequence, or some other consequence. Whether composed
of voluntary, semivoluntary, or mandated members, all formed groups
share certain commonalities.

Members of formed groups must be helped to understand why
they have been asked to come together and what they stand to gain
from the experience. They need to know what will be expected of
them, and what it is that they can expect from the worker and from
each other. They must be helped to define their common purpose, and
to identify their personal goals within the framework of that broader
purpose. The student must explain his/her function in helping them
to achieve the goals they have established. The understanding and acceptance of a shared purpose serves as the foundation for each person's
progression from a solitary individual to a member of a group that will
function as a mutual aid social system.

Drawing again on Jim's unsuccessful attempts to organize a hypertension support group through traditional approaches, let's assume
he would then be advised by the department's group work consultant
to reconceptualize his notion of formed groups and to integrate aspects of the approach to natural groups. On the day the clinic saw
hypertension patients, Jim would enter the waiting room, set down
the refreshments he had brought, and introduce himself as a social
work intern. He would tell the patients that he knew how stressful
waiting to see the doctor could be, and joke that the wait itself could
raise a person's blood pressure. A worker in this situation would express hope that he could assist them in helping each other deal with
the long wait, the feelings it was likely to evoke, and other issues related to their hypertension. Such an approach would help the patients—strangers to each other—draw themselves into discussion with
him about their feelings in the waiting room, their medical protocols,
and the related issues that Jim had hoped they would discuss as a
group. In an actual waiting room group described by a student in class,

the patients became so invested in the group experience that instead of leaving the hospital after seeing the doctor, they rejoined the other members for the remainder of the meeting.

By broadening his concept of how groups could be brought together, Jim could create structures through which people in shared, stressful circumstances could help each other.

Voluntary Membership. All of the groups discussed so far in this chapter have been composed of people who chose to be group members. They may have been recruited from direct contact, through referrals from their colleagues, or from public notices about the group being formed.

Even voluntary group members can be expected to have some ambivalence and feelings of caution (Garland, Jones, & Kolodny, 1976). This is especially true for the semi-volunteer who is there because of some external pressure. The person who is there at the insistence of a spouse is one such example. Even the most self-motivated members benefit from professional skills aimed at helping them become invested in the group experience. Each of the formed groups described in this chapter was helped to reach the point where work with natural groups may begin. It is natural for friends to celebrate milestones such as birthdays with each other, as in Jeannie's support group. It represents progress when acquaintances want to know more about each other's lives, as in Tom's parenting group. It is a sign of connection when members turn to each other for support around their vulnerabilities, as in Francine's planning group, and ultimately in Jim's group. The members entered the group with the hope and expectation that they could benefit from the experience. They remained in the group because their expectations were being met.

Mandatory Membership. Mandatory groups are those that members must attend in order to avoid a most undesirable alternative, usually a legal consequence. This could be a prison sentence for a drunk driving offense, or the removal of a child from the home because of parental abuse or neglect. It is common for students to feel awkward and intrusive when faced with such a seemingly resistant and frequently hostile membership. The student should remember and should point out to the members that at some level they have chosen to attend, and in all likelihood, would like to acquire behaviors that would remove the threat of the negative consequences they joined the group to avoid.

Students can help members engage in the group process by encouraging discussion of their feelings about being forced to attend and their feelings about not needing the group. The very reasons for their resistance may lead to the core of their problem. It can prove most helpful to work with the resistance, rather than fighting or ignoring it (Shulman, 1999). Students should point out that the reluctant members still have the choice of how they will spend the time within group meetings. Trimble (1994) tells his mandated male batterers that though they would rather not be in the group, once there, "no one can reach into your mind and heart and order a change. That's where you have complete control" (p. 262). Mandated members can recognize this as empowerment, and the potential power struggles between members and worker can be eased.

Groups Defined by Structure

Groups may often be defined by some aspect of the way they are structured. This section will discuss three commonly used structural descriptions of group types. These are closed groups, open-ended groups, and single session groups.

Closed Groups

Closed groups are those in which most members begin and end at the same time. Some groups have natural, predetermined time boundaries. Francine's holiday party planning committee could disband or change its purpose after the party occurred. Groups in school settings usually terminate at the conclusion of the school year. In other circumstances, groups may be scheduled for a certain number of sessions in the belief that goals can reasonably be met in that time.

An understanding of group development theory is critical for assessment and subsequent intervention in closed groups. A student must appreciate that the same piece of behavior exhibited by a member at the first meeting may have a different meaning at the seventh meeting, and may call for a different intervention. Knowledge of group development can also help a student depersonalize and even appreciate the normally difficult phases in the life of a group. For example, a comparison of developmental theories (Toseland & Rivas, 2001) reveals the widespread observation that relatively early in the life of the group, members will compete for status and influence, and will engage in some degree of testing behavior towards each other and towards the worker. If students know this, they will welcome this phenomenon as a sign of the group's progress rather than believe this represents the loss of their ability to control the group.

Tom's group may well have been in a testing stage. He was beginning to feel some frustration and irritation because the parents were not reading the assigned articles, and were not addressing the curriculum he had developed. On one level, these parents were following their own agenda of interest in each other, finding their places within

the group's social structure and locating where they were most comfortable with the group's range of behavioral norms. On another level,
the members may have been testing Tom's ability to let them control
their own group. If Tom were to insist that the members stick to the
agenda he had developed, he might fail the test, and eventually lose
members. He would not be the first professional in these circumstances
to conclude that the members were indeed unmotivated and hard to
reach, rather than recognizing that he was the one who found it hard
to listen. An understanding of group development could foster a more
successful outcome.

The cohesion that is fostered by the membership stability of closed
groups also creates an environment in which taboo subjects can be
explored in greater depth than in groups with changing membership.
The student needs to build on the trust and acceptance that can develop within a stable group to create a culture of open expression and
mutual support. Closed groups are more likely to reach this point than
those that have to deal with the disruption of members entering and
leaving from meeting to meeting.

Open-ended Groups

These are groups that may meet indefinitely, but with a changing
membership. People enter and leave throughout the life of the group.
The hypertension waiting room group was open-ended. Membership
changed as new patients began to use the clinic and other patients
were seen with decreasing frequency.

The benefits of open-ended groups include the often welcome
stimulation that comes from the entry of new members. Reviewing
the group's purpose for the new members helps the others to maintain a focus on the reason they are together. Continuing members can
serve as culture bearers and guide new individuals into membership
more quickly than it took the original individuals to become a group.

As recognized earlier, the disadvantages of this kind of group include greater difficulty in helping members develop trust and intimacy
with each other, and the loss of continuity of the issues being discussed. In open-ended groups, the group development momentum
referred to in the discussion of closed groups may be present (Schopler
& Galinsky, 1984), but may be less powerful.

Agencies may sometimes establish open-ended groups more because of financial reasons than for benefits to members. The availability of an ongoing group to which clients can be quickly referred is an
advantage for an agency dependent on funds from a managed care
arrangement. In addition, the possibility of a short-term membership

group experience may be the only option for people whose insurance coverage is only for a few sessions. Unfortunately, this may cause some members to terminate before they have reached the goals they had set for themselves.

Single-session Groups

Single-session groups are those that meet once for a specific, well-defined purpose. They are being increasingly used, especially in medical settings where people with a shared medical crisis can "air complaints, express fears, share information and get support" (Ebenstein, 1999, p. 49). However, single-session groups can be helpful in many situations; for instance, Gladstone and Reynolds (1997) describe their use to deal with stress reduction in the workplace.

This kind of group can be intense and meaningful in itself, and also can provide valuable recruitment opportunities for longer-term groups. If the members find the single meeting helpful, they may be motivated to enter into a continuing group experience. The student could even engage members in planning for such a group. Jim could have experimented with a single session hypertension information group as a way to find members for the group he was trying to organize.

Groups Defined by Content

Many group workers have been asked if their groups were "activity," or "discussion," or even "activity," or "therapy." Both of these are false dichotomies, since activity groups are not silent, and dialogue is not the only path to therapy. This section will examine major aspects of groups described as either discussion groups or activity groups.

Discussion Groups

Social work education includes content on communication in general, and the interview process in particular. The special dimension of communication in groups, however, is the need to focus on helping the members to communicate with each other. It is common for members to begin their group experience by addressing their remarks to the worker, and the student must learn to redirect the communication flow. Group work is not casework with many people at the same time, and it is the mutual aid that results from members interacting with each other that makes that difference. Tom did not realize how fortunate it was that the parents in his group had reached that point.

Activity Groups

Activities serve to promote interaction, creativity, and to develop feelings of personal mastery. Middleman and Wood (1990) say of activity that it

> is the driving force for whatever words are exchanged. The talk arises from the action, is about the action, and is mediated by it . . . some persons know what to do with each other as long as they are busy with play, with a project, or even with chores. (p. 135)

Activity groups are particularly effective with children and other populations whose verbal abilities are not well developed. They may also serve as an effective starting point for work with people who are not yet ready to directly address the painful and possibly to them, shameful, problems they face. For such people, it may be easier to start a relationship around pleasurable experiences rather than focusing on hurts and deficits.

Activities are frequently central to socialization groups which aim to help members attain higher levels of social functioning. The activities can convert the group into a microcosm of daily life. As such, they provide opportunities for engaging people in the group process, and helping them express and understand the aspects of themselves that emerge in the course of natural human interaction. Finally, activities offer pleasurable ways to grow and develop.

Conclusion

Field instructors must help students to understand the many ways groups can be formulated, and the implications of these for the group's working agreement and the group worker's practice interventions. Such an understanding provides both guidelines and options for effective practice. Too often, we hear it said that a certain person is not suited for a group. That cannot be, since all of life occurs with other people. The challenge to students is to determine which kinds of groups can be most helpful to the people they seek to serve.

References

Barker, R. L. (1987). *The social work dictionary*. Silver Spring, MD: NASW Press.

Bass, D. (1995). Runaways and homeless youths. In R. L. Edwards (Ed.-in-Chief), *Encyclopedia of social work* (19th ed., pp. 2060-2068). Washington, DC: NASW Press.

Ebenstein, H. (1999). Single-session groups: Issues for social workers. *So-*

cial Work with Groups, 21(1/2), 49-60.

Ephross, P. H., & Vassil, T. V. (1988). *Groups that work: Structure and process*. New York: Columbia University Press.

Falk, H. (1995). Central characteristics of social work with groups. In R. Kurland & R. Salmon (Eds.), *Group work practice in a troubled society* (pp. 63-72). Binghampton, NY: Haworth.

Frey, L. A. (1966). *Use of groups in the health field*. NewYork: National Association of Social Workers.

Garland, J. (1986).The relationship between group work and group therapy. In M. Parnes (Ed.), *Proceedings of the annual group work symposium. Innovations in social group work: Feedback from practice to theory* (pp. 17-28). Binghamton, NY: Haworth.

Garland, J., Jones, H., & Kolodny, R. (1976). A model for stages of development in social work groups. In S. Bernstein (Ed.), *Explorations in group work: Essays in theory and practice* (pp. 17-71). Boston: Charles River Books.

Gladstone, J., & Reynolds, T. (1997). Single session group work intervention in response to employee stress during workforce transformation. *Social Work with Groups, 20*(1), 33-49.

Hartford, M. E., & Lawton, S. (1997). Groups for the socialization to old age. In J. K. Parry (Ed.), *From prevention to wellness through group work* (pp. 33-45). Binghamton, NY: Haworth.

Kuechler, C. F. (1997). Psychoeducational groups: A model for recovery and celebration of the self. In J. K. Parry (Ed.), *From prevention to wellness through group work* (pp. 47-59). Binghamton, NY: Haworth.

Middleman, R. R., & Wood, G. G. (1990). *Skills for direct practice in social work*. New York: Columbia University Press.

Pappell, C. P., & Rothman, B. (1962). Social group work models: Possession and heritage. *Journal of Education for Social Work, 2*, 66-77.

Pappell, C. P., & Rothman, B. (1980). Relating the mainstream model of social work with groups to group psychotherapy and the structured group approach. *Social Work with Groups, 3*(2), 5-23.

Schopler, J. H., & Galinsky, M. J. (1984). Meeting practice needs: Conceptualizing the open-ended group. *Social Work with Groups, 7*(2), 3-21.

Shulman, L. (1999). *The skills of helping individuals, families, groups and communities* (4th ed.). Itasca, IL: F.E. Peacock.

Toseland, R. W., & Rivas, R. F. (2001). *An introduction to group work practice* (4th ed.). Neeedham Heights, MA: Allyn & Bacon.

Trimble, D. (1994). Confronting responsibility: Men who batter their wives. In A. Gitterman & L. Shulman (Eds.), *Mutual aid groups, vulnerable populations, and the life cycle* (pp. 257-271). New York: Columbia University Press.

Wasserman, H., & Danforth, H. E. (1988). *The human bond.* NY: Springer.

Wayne, J. (1979). A group work model to reach isolated mothers: Preventing child abuse. *Social Work with Groups, 2*(1), 7-18.

Chapter 5 | Education for Practice Informed by Theory: Making Optimal Use of Learning and Teaching Structures and Tools

The daily pressures of agency life can easily divert attention and energy from the educational goal of teaching students to engage in practice that is consciously informed by values, knowledge, and theory. Field instructors feel the need to teach the content to get the job done (Rogers & McDonald, 1995), and beginning students seek and more quickly grasp the how-to skills than they do the theoretical frameworks that guide professional practice (Reynolds, 1942). Many students are not even certain critical analysis and application of theory makes any difference in what social workers do to help clients resolve problems (Vayda & Bogo, 1991, p. 271).

Yet, professional education must go beyond job training. Its purpose is to teach the conceptual foundation upon which all professional activities are built. Social work students must acquire knowledge that can be transferred to the range of problems, settings, and populations that make up the social work profession. It is not sufficient to teach skills and techniques without the theoretical framework within which to make judgments about their use.

Though there is inescapable logic to the goal of integrating theory and practice, it is very difficult for even the most committed teacher to do. Social work educators around the world identify this as one of their greatest challenges (Raskin, Skolnik, & Wayne, 1991; Skolnik, Wayne, & Raskin, 1999), and American field education experts agree that the theoretical content of classroom courses does not fit well with the practical demands of field education (Raskin, 1994). Efforts to strengthen relations between the academic and practice arenas began in the earliest days of social work education and continue today (Schneck, 1991).

Students as well as field and classroom teachers often reinforce the perception of the gap between the academic and practice arenas. Field instructors are known to complain that students are not being taught the skills they need for practice in their specific settings, and classroom teachers often express dismay about the lack of field support for the conceptualized practice taught in class. Students of group work practice indicate that classroom teachers need to add more practical components to the curriculum, and that field instructors do not teach theory as well as they give practical advice (Wayne, Richards, & Raskin, 1997).

Even when immediately relevant concepts are taught in class, beginning students often have difficulty recognizing their relatedness to their practice. Even adult learners, within the framework of their professional education, may be at Piaget's pre-conservation stage (Piaget & Inhelder, 1969, p. 97). In this stage, the learner is unable to recognize the constant invariant in a system of transformations. Applied to group work education, this would explain beginning students' inability to recognize group dynamics and processes when they get acted out through behaviors that are different than the examples offered in class. The occasional frustration field instructors and classroom teachers feel with each other may be a result, in part, of the student as a weak link between the educational arenas.

This chapter focuses on elevating group work training to group work education. It examines the benefits and limitations of differently organized field assignments, experiences, and supervisory structures and offers educationally focused reporting formats to be used as teaching tools.

Ways for Students to Experience Groups

Since the early days of social work education, social workers were aware that practice could only be learned by doing (Cassidy, 1982, p. 199). The learning that comes from single or co-leadership group work assignments can be augmented with observational experiences and role-play. The following discussion examines the benefits and limitations of these structures and activities.

Single Leadership of Groups

If the best way to learn to practice is by practicing, then the best way to learn competent autonomous practice is to practice autonomously. Therefore, it is vital that every field experience includes a single leadership group work assignment.

The student may begin responsibility for the group in its planning and formative stage, at the point of its first meeting, or may take over an established group from another worker. Each of these are legitimate options, the selection of which is best based on an assessment of the students learning needs. Understandably, the decision of where to begin is often based, as well, on the reality of agency circumstances.

Single leadership fosters total involvement in the experience, and requires students to make professional judgments and decisions based on the totality of circumstances. They must rely on the combination of their growing knowledge base and the sense data that comes from their intuitive and affective responses to the situations and people they face (Cassidy, 1982). There is a unique personal component to this multidimensional learning that is best fostered by practicing as the group's single worker.

Co-leadership of Groups

Co-leadership is common in group work practice, and its use has been addressed in the literature (Kolodny, 1980; Shulman, 1999; Toseland & Rivas, 2001). This section begins with a review of the educational benefits and costs of co-leadership, and then identifies areas that must be addressed in order to take full advantage of the benefits.

Co-leadership offers opportunities to learn through modeling, especially when students are working with professionals whose group work skills are more advanced than their own (Shulman, 1999). Co-leaders can help each other achieve greater self-awareness by providing feedback about their performance in the group. Through joint problem solving, they can be helped to sharpen their assessment and interventive skills.

The support of compatible co-leadership can lessen anxiety for the novice, and lessen the strain of dealing with the difficult and painful moments within the group (Galinsky & Schopler, 1980). It allows students to test their new professional behaviors without feeling solely responsible for the results (Shulman, 1999).

The potential limitations of co-leadership include fewer opportunities and less need for the student to develop the full range of interventive skills. For example, the student who comes to rely on a co-leader to consistently set limits for the group, can remain the group nurturer or good cop. The need for co-leaders to focus on and adjust their respective roles in the group can divert attention from the needs of the group members. Finally, and perhaps most seriously, there may be a reduced need for students to practice making independent judgments based on the integration of their new knowledge and personal responses. This is especially true when students co-lead with senior practitioners to whom they feel deferential.

When planning a co-leadership experience for educational purposes, the following interrelated factors must be considered.

How is co-leadership being defined?

The term co-leadership implies two individuals with equal responsibility and status. Equal responsibility can take the form of different but complementary leadership roles. Quite often, however, co-leaders are different but unequal, much like senior and junior counselors at camp. At times, a student may even be assigned to a quasi-observer role. There is value in each of these approaches, but whichever one it is meant to be must be clear to both parties. They must clarify their relative roles and functions, and communicate these to the group members.

What are the student's learning needs?

Inexperienced, anxious students may request to begin with a co-leader for all the supports identified earlier. However, some believe that the ability to co-lead is itself an advanced skill and should be learned only after a student has developed basic group work skills through practice with their own group. These conflicting views point to the complexity of the issue. Co-leadership could be helpful to students who learn better from concrete experiences than intellectual concepts. For the student that just doesn't get it, even after weeks of discussing an aspect of practice, co-leading could be helpful.

What is the nature of the group? What is in its best interest?

There are circumstances in which group factors point to the need for co-leadership. Such circumstances could include a group with membership of those with physical limitations or with impulse control problems. At times, mainstreaming a special needs person succeeds only if there is more than one professional present to deal with the difficult situations that could arise. It is not in the student's or the group's best interest to be understaffed, and co-leadership may be the best solution.

With whom will the co-leadership occur?

Students can co-lead with a more senior social worker, possibly their field instructor; with a professional from another discipline; with a paraprofessional; or with another social work student. Each of these options has different implications for the learning experience and how the field instructor can best teach from the group assignment.

For example, co-leading with an experienced professional maximizes opportunities for the student to learn through modeling. However, this approach is likely to increase the student's dependency on the co-leader and inhibit the ability to develop his/her own professional style. Co-leading with the person to whom one is directly accountable will also inhibit the inclination to risk, and thus, to learn from mistakes. If a student does co-lead with a senior person, there must be a plan for the student to assume an increasingly self-directing role as the experience progresses. If a student is co-leading with someone other than a social worker, it is usually because of a special contribution that person can make, as in the case of co-leading a diabetes support group with a nurse. However, there are times when such a person brings the outlook and values of a different professional culture as in the following example.

A student in a group work class once reported co-leading a "feelings" group with a teacher in an elementary school. When eight year old Billy began to loudly express anger at another youngster, and did not quiet down as the teacher demanded, she asked him to leave the room. She later explained to the social work student that the boy needed to experience consequences for his inappropriate behavior and in addition, he was spoiling the group process. All of this seemed logical to the student until discussion in her group work class pointed to the fact that the purpose of the group was to help youngsters learn how to recognize and deal with feelings, including anger. The class talked about the value of exploring the incident with Billy, and helping him and other children relate the event to the purpose of the group. Billy could have been asked what was getting him so angry and then been helped to find more constructive behaviors to use in the situation. In this case, modeling the teacher's intervention would have worked against the student's education as a social group worker.

The above discussion concluded with advice to the student about how to handle her co-leader. Fortunately, the teacher with whom she working was open to the new point of view the student offered, and the incident with Billy was revisited. Sadly, there are instances when this kind of arrangement has a less successful conclusion.

Co-leading with another social work student presents the greatest opportunity for equal co-leadership status. Even then, prior experience and personality traits will influence respective roles. The students will have to recognize and openly deal with this as they develop their working relationship with each other.

What are the educational structures and opportunities that surround the group experience?

Co-leadership cannot be viewed as single leadership through two different people. The differences between workers can enhance the group experience, but may also create tensions within the working relationship. In order to heighten the positive effects and lessen the negative ones, co-leaders need to commit time outside of group meetings to discuss their respective perceptions and thoughts about their shared experience. They need to be able to question each other's interventions, and to express and explore feelings about their work together. Meeting five minutes before each group session to discuss what they will do that day is not enough.

Optimally, co-leaders should be supervised together. To supervise one co-leader without the other is to overlook the reciprocity of their roles. Almost all classroom teachers have had situations in which a student complains about the approach of a co-leader who is supervised by someone other than the student's field instructor. This often leads to discussions of ways for the student to handle the co-leader. Such discussions, in effect, convert the co-leader from a professional partner to another group member who must be helped to learn new behaviors. Aside from the general unpleasantness of such a conflict-ridden situation, it also draws attention and energy away from the purpose of the group work assignment, which is to learn group work practice. A problem such as this could be mitigated through joint supervision. Even if the agency's administrative structure makes joint supervision difficult to implement, it is in the student's best educational interest to make every effort to make special arrangements.

Observation of Groups

There are circumstances in which observing a group can be very useful. It is especially valuable when group work assignments are not immediately available and students begin course work without an ongoing group work experience to relate to class content, or to use as the basis for course assignments. Students may lose many of the benefits of classroom learning without the opportunity to apply theoretical concepts to concrete situations. This may be especially important for students who learn primarily through inductive processes, or, "first engaging in experiences from which they can subsequently generalize to formulate concepts" (Hamilton & Else, 1983, p. 27). Observing a group can offer many of the same advantages as co-leadership. Observation provides opportunity to learn through modeling, and can reduce anxiety for overanxious students whose fantasies about group work may be far worse than any reality they will face.

Under any circumstances, observation should be considered as an ancillary, rather than a central assignment. Sheafor and Jenkins (1982) state that students must "ultimately advance beyond passive observation . . . and work with clients of their own." They further add that exclusive reliance on any passive approach to learning has marked limitations, including "the destruction of initiative and curiosity" (p. 218). Observation can rarely evoke the necessary depth of emotional reaction to group members and events that would foster the integration of personal responses and professional practice. Unless emotional responses are fully accessible, the student's experience is more intellectual than holistic, and does not meet the purpose of the practicum. Most importantly, relationship is the key component of all direct practice, and an observed group work experience provides no opportunity for the interactions through which relationship is built.

Participation in Group Simulations or Role-plays

In a group work role-play situation, a group scenario is developed and individuals act the part of real or fictional others. Munson (1983) notes the growth of role-play use in education and supervision, and parallels it with the popularity of psychodrama in therapy.

Role-play can be conducted in many different ways. It can be used in supervision, either spontaneously or by plan. The field instructor could assume the role of a particular group member so that the student can rehearse a range of responses in order to find how best to intervene (Shulman, 1994). Using a role reversal approach, a student can assume the role of a difficult member in order to gain insight and understanding of that person's point of view (Ephross & Vassil, 1988).

Role-play has excellent potential for use in group supervision, when some or all of the participants create or re-create member roles. Students can assume worker, co-worker, or member roles, and within this shared frame of reference, can discuss their various interpretations of the same experience and solutions to perceived problems.

Munson (1983) identifies a limitation of the extended use of role-play and simulations, similar to one discussed in relation to observation. He says such "exercises limit the depth of feelings that can be expressed, especially when the participants have limited experience with the type of material under exploration" (p. 229). Role-play is very well received by students. It is a lively exercise that gives students the opportunity to try out new professional behaviors in situations where there are minimal consequences for errors.

Supervisory Structures

In order to promote the integration of theory and practice, supervision must serve as a vehicle for expanding knowledge and for helping students to apply that knowledge to practice. The field instructor serves as a resource for new information as well as a guide through a problem-solving process. Supervision should be built upon a collaboratively developed learning contract that includes learning objectives, the activities designed to meet the objectives, how progress will be evaluated, and the roles and expectations of the parties involved (Hamilton & Else, 1983; Wijnberg & Schwartz, 1977; Wilson, 1981). A clearly articulated learning contract can foster an open, trusting relationship through which the field instructor can both support and challenge the student.

The learning contract should also address the boundaries of the personal material that will be addressed. Purely academic subjects focus primarily on cognitive growth, but social work education reaches for the whole person. Personal, emotional factors that impact professional performance cannot be fully discussed in the classroom, but are legitimately part of the supervisory process (Grossman, Levine-Jordano, & Shearer, 1991). Beginning group work students, for example, could be asked about their past experiences and current feelings about groups, the roles they tend to assume as members, and the vulnerabilities they might have as a group worker. After practice has begun, the student who demonstrates limited potential to develop the self-awareness necessary for professional practice, or the student for whom self-awareness is not enough to bring about satisfactory professional development should be advised to seek help outside of the supervisory relationship.

Most student supervision occurs through one-to-one meetings of the supervisor and the student under supervision. Group supervision, when used, is usually offered in addition to, rather than instead of individual supervision (Kadushin, 1992). Each of these structures offers advantages, and learning can be maximized through a combination of both. Live supervision, an approach used most widely in supervision of family therapy, has value for group work education, and will be included in this discussion.

Individual Supervision

The traditional supervisory structure is the one-to-one regularly scheduled weekly meeting, lasting anywhere from one to two hours. Most of what has been written about this form of supervision applies to education for all social work methods, and there is little to add about its specific use for supervision of group work practice. The special aspects of one-to-one group work supervision lie in the content about group work practice and the tailored uses of reporting formats as teaching tools.

A major advantage of individual supervision is the opportunity it offers to focus on a student's educational needs without concern for others in the group. It is a helpful vehicle for addressing issues related to professional development that are too personal or too specific to be discussed in a group situation. Since a major portion of a student's education occurs within groups, opportunities for individual attention provide a needed balance to the overall educational experience. For these reasons, most social work programs consider individual supervision to be the core of field education.

There is some concern that the one-to-one tutorial approach could foster dependency and over-identification with agency culture, while discouraging critical thinking and creative problem solving (Marshack & Glassman, 1991). Additional drawbacks are the absence of the benefits of learning with and from peers.

Group Supervision

Group supervision is defined as simultaneous supervision of two or more students, though the most common number is four or five (Kadushin, 1992). The unique benefits of groups identified in chapter 2 apply as well to group supervision, no matter what the social work method being taught. These benefits include opportunities for students to universalize their experiences and to receive emotional support for the difficult work they face. They benefit from the stimulation and new perspectives of problem solving with others and can learn more about themselves as developing professionals from peer feedback. They may also enjoy feelings of increased safety and empowerment through their bonding with other students.

Group supervision can be especially powerful for teaching group work practice. It creates a valuable opportunity to help students recognize the parallels between the dynamics and components of the supervisory group and the groups with which they work. Kadushin (1992) recognizes that for those supervised, "Participation in the group becomes the source of learning about group interaction, group process, group operations, and . . . feelings about group membership" (p. 404). Kadushin also recognizes that in order to maximize the benefits of group supervision, the supervisor must have group work skills.

To take advantage of group supervision for experiential learning, the learning contract/working agreement must recognize that the group, at times, will serve as a reference point for the concepts being discussed. The field instructor, however, must seek to maintain an optimum balance between intellectual and experiential learning. It is best, therefore, that the group remains a reference rather than focal point of attention. If the group's own processes become the primary content, feelings of self-consciousness and emotional reactions may interfere with the learners' abilities to objectively examine intellectual material and its application to their practice. This focus could also evoke feelings that are too personal to discuss within the boundaries of the students' working agreement with each other and that are better left for discussion in individual supervision.

Some field instructors may be anxious about the empowerment for students of group supervision and avoid it lest they feel ganged up on by students who instructors fear would turn the meetings into gripe sessions. Such negative feelings, however, should be used as grist for the educational mill. The field instructor could use the opportunity to model open, honest discussion of conflict-ridden areas and could engage students in a problem-solving process that can be replicated in their own practices.

There are many parallels between group supervision and models of group work practice. For example, group supervision shares many aspects of educational groups. As described in Chapter 4, educational groups both provide knowledge and help their members incorporate and translate that knowledge into new behaviors. That is also a goal of supervision. Supervisory sessions also can be based on a teacher-centered or group-centered approach. In the former, the field instructor is central to the supervisory group and takes major responsibility for offering practice-related content. In the latter, the students as a group are central, and they take major responsibility for agenda setting and peer teaching. When the student group is central the field instructor focuses on promoting constructive group interaction and serves as an educational resource. In any approach, supervisory sessions could either focus on a single student's group or on a generalized topic of the day.

Given the range of student learning styles, the varied use of these and other formats, provides greater opportunities than would be available with the consistent use of a single approach. Group development theory should serve as a guide for making judgments about teaching interventions in supervisory sessions (Kaplan, 1991). Issues such as authority and trust are linked to group movement, and the field instructor must assess these and other factors before deciding on how to proceed. Students and field instructors could identify additional parallels between groups for supervision and for practice as their continuing experiences move them to new levels of knowing, understanding, and questioning.

Live Supervision

The basic components of live supervision are the direct observation and instruction of the supervised student while engaged in practice. The field instructor or team of supervisors observes the student either in a group meeting, or through a one-way mirror. From outside the room, supervision occurs through a telephone message, a note, the student's earphone or a knock on the meeting room door to enter or to call the student out (Kadushin, 1992).

Live supervision has both advantages and disadvantages. The primary advantages are the opportunities for direct observation of the student's practice, and for offering on the spot practical advice. Of course, such an arrangement could only occur with the members' prior knowledge and permission. Members could be invited to participate in the discussion and evaluation of the interventions they have experienced, and in planning which ones they believe would be helpful and why. In spite of the intrusive nature of this approach, in our experience, group members have expressed their appreciation of the additional attention they receive. The disadvantages of live supervision include the interruption of the student's thought processes and the interaction between the group and the student. An agency administrator would also consider the cost of dedicating a team of professionals (if that were the case) to one professional encounter.

This unusual approach, if used selectively, could add a valuable dimension to the learning experience. Its very unorthodoxy could be helpful at a point when the student or the group is stuck and traditional methods of supervision and practice have not succeeded in moving the group forward. Interrupting a dysfunctional process can help to change it.

Aside from the cost and cumbersome nature of live supervision, it would not be in the student's best interest to do this on a regular basis. As stated earlier, students need the opportunity to exercise judgment and to correct their own mistakes.

Methods of Bringing Group Process Into Supervision

Direct practice is reported through a range of formats including written process recordings, audio and visual tapes, logs, and summaries. Recording is used to insure appropriate client care, to educate and evaluate supervised students, and for agency administrative purposes. This section will focus on the use of reporting approaches for group work education in the field.

Process Recording

A process recording is as exact and faithful an account as possible of a professional encounter with a client system. Graybeal and Ruff (1995) offer a broad definition of process recording that includes verbal accounts, written procedures, audiotaping, videotaping, and live observation. In spite of technological advances, the primary tool in the training of social work students remains the old-fashioned written process recording (Neuman & Friedman, 1997).

Various guidelines for the use of process recording (Neuman & Friedman, 1997; Royse, Dhooper & Rompf, 1999; Wilson, 1981) include sections in which students are asked to add their gut-level feelings about the practice encounter and their interpretation of what occurred, using theory to explain client behaviors and their choice of professional interventions. Wayne and Carter (1983) propose a five-part recording guideline beginning with writing a statement of goals and plans for an upcoming meeting before it occurs. After the meeting, students are asked to write as exact and faithful an account as possible, to interpret the meaning of what occurred, and to evaluate their own performance. They are then asked to determine which goals were met, which ones needed to be changed as the meeting unfolded, and to renew the recording cycle by identifying their goals and plans for the next meeting.

Guidelines are best used when they are adapted to students' changing learning needs. Any written section could be stressed and elaborated upon as indicated. If goal formulation is high on the teaching agenda, a student may be asked to expand the discussion of goals for individuals and the group as a whole. If the student needs help in self-awareness, he/she may be asked to focus on the incidents that evoked a personal reaction and to analyze how feelings influenced the intervention. If a student is working with more than one group, he/she may be asked to describe in detail a particular kind of interaction as it occurred in any of her groups rather than a full process recording of any one meeting. The student and the field instructor can be creative and flexible in the use of this teaching tool.

The literature about process recording frequently refers to its reconstruction of an interview rather than of a group meeting (Dwyer & Urbanowski, 1966; Graybeal & Ruff, 1995; Neuman & Friedman, 1997; Wilson, 1981). This is consistent with data indicating that students and field instructors use process recordings far less frequently for group work than for casework supervision (Wayne & Garland, 1990; Wayne et al., 1997). Yet, they are as critical to group work as to casework education.

The sheer volume of activity and dialogue in a group meeting leads many students to believe they would be unable to re-create a verbatim account of what had occurred. In actuality, it is not necessary to include the meeting's every word. Kurland and Salmon (1998) recognize that "100% accuracy is impossible and is not really the aim. Rather, one strives to describe what took place in a group meeting as fully and as best as one can recollect" (p. 205). The most significant interactions and incidents that need to be explored for educational or practice purposes should be written in greater detail than the summary descriptions that link parts of the meeting to each other. Shulman (1994) describes this expansion and contraction of meeting details as an "accordion" style of recording. He points to the importance of elaborating on the group processes that occur at the beginning and ending of meetings.

The passage of time can be helpful in sharpening the student's identification and memory of the meeting's more significant events. Immediately following the meeting, the student should jot down dialogue and incidents that stand out in memory. The recording in its entirety could be written a day or two later. The notes will jog the student's recall, and the recording could more easily be written without superfluous details that would distract from the session's major moments and themes.

Process recording with co-leaders. Process recording with co-leaders is a variant of the usual form of process recording. Each co-leader could write a process recording of the meeting and then compare their recollections. This process could help them to capitalize on their differences by broadening each of their perspectives and encouraging exploration that could result in enhanced practice. It would also help them to understand the frame of reference each is bringing to their study and discussion of the group, and deepen the level of their communication with each other.

Process recording from a member's perspective. Another variant is process recording from a member's perspective. Students who are having an especially difficult time assessing or empathizing with a certain member could be asked to write a process recording from the perspective of that member's experience in the group. This parallels the role-play approach of acting the part of a particular member. One student reported to his field instructor that this technique helped deepen his understanding of a group member who was having relationship problems with peers and who was consistently challenging him. Seeing the meeting through the member's eyes increased his empathy for this troubled youngster. Although he reported a skewed perspective of the meeting as a whole, he concluded that the temporary awkwardness was a small price to pay for the new perspective that increased his effectiveness with the youngster, and ultimately with the group as a whole.

Summary Recording

Although detailed process recording is invaluable in the study of professional interventions, it is usually unrealistic to expect them to be written for each meeting of every group. Meeting summaries take less time to write and have their value as well. A summary of a meeting should contain the basic information of what happened at the meeting and how it happened. More specifically, it should include the meeting date and attendance and then move on to the meeting's agenda or activities, topics of discussion, themes that emerged and actions or decisions that were taken. Summary writing requires the student to gain a perspective that transcends specific incidents and interactions. A sequential review of summaries can be most helpful in assessing group movement and development.

Logs and Journals

Logs and journals are similar to personal diaries that focus on reactions to daily life. Students could be asked to write about the moments in group meetings that were the most gratifying, challenging, anxiety-provoking, or confusing. They could then be asked to study and evaluate the part their emotional responses played in their choice of professional interventions. Students who are asked to keep logs for any of their classroom courses could be asked to integrate that content into their field logs as well. This type of recording fosters the integration of personal and professional self necessary for sensitive, informed practice.

Audiotapes and Videotapes

In addition to providing greater accuracy than recall in the recounting of a group meeting, tapes provide access to more subtle elements of interaction such as tone of voice, the rhythm of the interactions, and with videotapes, body language. By studying these additional dimensions of personal expression, students can be helped to communicate and understand member interactions more deeply and fully than before. The spoken word alone can sometimes divert attention away from true meanings. People don't always say what they mean or what they are feeling. When a teaching objective is to help a student tune in to nonverbal interaction, a videotape could be muted, and the group meeting analyzed through body language, movements, and facial expression

Taping can occur only with the full knowledge and consent of all the parties involved. Students should explain the purpose of the taping and how it will be used. In most instances, any self-consciousness the taping creates dissipates as the meeting progresses.

Combined Use of Process Recordings and Tapes

Students can be helped to measure their ability to accurately reconstruct group meetings, by both taping and writing a process recording of a session. They could then compare what they wrote to what actually occurred, and consider the educational and practical significance of what they had distorted or forgotten.

Direct Observation by Field Instructor

The field instructor can learn about the student's practice by direct observation, either in the room with the group as it meets, or observing through a one-way mirror. The benefits of direct observation are akin to viewing a tape, though the absence of video equipment could be less stressful for some members. It is also relatively easy to do in the event of equipment not being readily available. A disadvantage of live observation in comparison to video taping is the inability to stop the process at any point and replay important moments. If the field instructor uses this approach, measures should be taken to keep his presence as unobtrusive as possible.

Reconstructing Group Cues

A field instructor relying on the student to reconstruct the events and feelings of the group meeting, could bring reminders of the meeting into supervisory sessions (Glassman & Kates, 1988). For example, supervision could be held in the room in which the meeting occurred. The seating arrangement could be replicated, and the student could be asked to sit in the place that a particular member sat when a certain incident under discussion occurred. These and other cues could trigger memories that enrich supervisory sessions.

Conclusion

The purpose of field education is to help students engage in practice that is informed by knowledge and theory. This chapter has offered a range of structures through which students can experience group work practice and through which supervision can occur.

References

Cassidy, H. (1982). Structuring field learning experiences. In B.W. Sheafor & L. E. Jenkins (Eds.), *Quality field instruction in social work* (pp. 198-214). New York: Longman.

Dwyer, M., & Urbanowski, M. (1966). Student process recording: A plea for structure. *Social Casework, 46*(5), 284-286.

Ephross, P. H., & Vassil, T. V. (1988). *Groups that work: Structure and process*. New York: Columbia University Press.

Galinsky, M. J., & Schopler, J. H. (1980). Structuring co-leadership in social work training. *Social Work with Groups, 3*(4), 51-63.

Glassman, U., & Kates, L. (1988). Strategies or group work field instruction. *Social Work with Groups, 11*(1/2), 111-124.

Graybeal, C. T., & Ruff, E. (1995). Process recording: It's more than you think. *Journal of Social Work Education, 31*, 169-181.

Grossman, B., Levine-Jordano, N., & Shearer, P. (1991). Working with students' emotional reactions in the field: An education framework. In D. Schneck, B. Grossman, & U. Glassman (Eds.), *Field education in social work: Contemporary issues and trends* (pp. 205-216). Dubuque, IA: Kendall/Hunt.

Hamilton, N., & Else, J. F. (1983). *Designing field education: Philosophy, structure, and process*. Springfield, IL: Charles C. Thomas.

Kadushin, A. (1992). *Supervision in social work*. New York: Columbia University Press.

Kaplan, T. (1991). A model for group supervision for social work: Implications for the profession. In D. Schneck, B. Grossman, & U. Glassman (Eds.), *Field education in social work: Contemporary issues and trends* (pp. 141-148). Dubuque, IA: Kendall/Hunt.

Kolodny, R. (1980). The dilemma of co-leadership. *Social Work with Groups*, *3*(4), 31-34.

Kurland, R., & Salmon, R. (1998). *Teaching a methods course in social work with groups*. Alexandria, VA: Council on Social Work Education.

Marshack, E., & Glassman, U. (1991). Innovative models for field instruction: Departing from traditional methods. In D. Schneck, B. Grossman, & U. Glassman (Eds.), *Field education in social work: Contemporary Issues and Trends* (pp. 84-95). Dubuque, IA: Kendall/Hunt.

Munson, C. E. (1983). *An introduction to clinical social work supervision*. Binghamton, NY: Haworth.

Neuman, K., & Friedman, B. (1997). Process recordings: Fine-tuning an old instrument. *Journal of Social Work Education*, *33*, 237-243.

Piaget, J., & Inhelder, B. (1969). *The psychology of the child*. New York: Basic Books.

Raskin, M. (1994). The Delphi study in field instruction revisited: Expert consensus on issues and research priorities. *Journal of Social Work Education*, *30*, 75-89.

Raskin, M., Skolnik, L., & Wayne, J. (1991). An international perspective of field instruction in social work education. *Journal of Social Work Education*, *27*, 258-270.

Reynolds, B. (1942). *Learning and teaching in the practice of social work*. New York: Russell & Russell.

Rogers, G., & McDonald, L. P. (1995). Expedience over education: Teaching methods used by field instructors. *The Clinical Supervisor*, *13*(2), 79-95.

Royse, D., Dhooper, S., & Rompf, E. (1999). *Field instruction: A guide for social work students*. New York: Addison Wesley Longman.

Schneck, D. (1991). Ideal and reality in field education. In D. Schneck, B. Grossman, & U. Glassman (Eds.). *Field education in social work: Contemporary Issues and Trends* (pp. 17-35). Dubuque, IA: Kendall/Hunt.

Sheafor, B.W. & Jenkins, L. E. (1982). Preface. In S.W. Sheafor & L. E. Jenkins (Eds.), *Quality field instruction in social work* (pp. ix-xii). New York: Longman.

Shulman, L. (1994). *Interactional supervision*. Washington, DC: NASW Press.

Shulman, L. (1999). *The skills of helping individuals, families, groups and communities* (4th ed.). Itasca, IL: F.E. Peacock.

Skolnik, L., Wayne, J., & Raskin, M. (1999). International field curricula. *International Journal of Social Work*, *42*(4), 471-483.

Toseland, R.W., & Rivas, R. F. (2001). *An introduction to group work practice* (4th ed.). Neeedham Heights, MA: Allyn & Bacon.

Vayda, E., & Bogo, M. (1991). A teaching model to unite classroom and field. *Journal of Social Work Education*, *27*(3), 271-278.

Wayne, J., & Carter, D. (1983). A recording model to promote independent learning. In J. Wayne, A. Eisenberg, & T. Zimmerman (Eds.), *Readings for new field instructors* (pp. 67-78). Lexington, MA: Ginn.

Wayne, J., & Garland, J. (1990). Group work education in the field: The state of the art. *Social Work with Groups, 13*(2), 95-109.

Wayne, J., Richards, M., & Raskin, M. (1997). *Group work education: The student perspective*. Paper presented at the Council on Social Work Education Annual Program Meeting, Chicago, IL.

Wijnberg, M. H., & Schwartz, M. C. (1977). Models of student supervision: The apprentice, growth, and role systems models. *Journal of Education for Social Work, 13*(3), 107-113.

Wilson, S. J. (1981). *Field instruction: Techniques for supervisors*. New York: Free Press.

Chapter 6 | Understanding the Student: Frameworks for Assessment

Start where the client is! Thousands of social work students have heard this mantra as they met with their field instructors and wondered where to begin with their new assignment. This simple wisdom has often helped to move them forward, from wondering what to say first to seeing the person-in-environment as the basis of assessment and planning. This wise phrase is probably repeated throughout the field work experience, whenever students seem to lose their focus.

Therefore, it should come as no surprise that when field instructors themselves wonder how to approach students, the best advice is to start where the student is. When working with clients, this principle directs us to consider both unique and universal qualities that bring clients to the attention of workers. Similarly, starting where the student is enables field instructors to tailor field experiences to both the special characteristics and shared qualities of each learner. Just as with clients, understanding students' reality in the early stages of the field practicum is a complex affair.

Field instructors can approach their preparation process through a variety of entry points. This chapter proposes three areas for exploration:

- Common fears in approaching practice with groups.
- Tuning in to students' perspectives on practice with groups.
- Stages of learning applied to practice with groups.

The first section elaborates on students' fears as they try to meet group members "where they are." This section proposes possible sources and meanings of common fears as well as strategies for helping students deal with their concerns, many of which may be shared with field instructors. The second section presents tuning in techniques to assist field instructors in preparing for work with each student. This process adds depth to field instructors' own examination of feelings about working with groups, as discussed in chapter 3. The final section uses a developmental approach for assessing student learning and planning appropriate teaching strategies and interventions. These three areas can be used separately or interwoven as a framework in the assessment process.

Common Fears of Students in Approaching Practice with Groups

While most students approach group assignments with excitement and anticipation, they also bring fears and worries. These concerns can come from a variety of sources, including limited classroom preparation for group work in the field, difficult past group experiences, and generalized worries about field work performance. The worker's lament: "So many of them and only one of me!" (Shulman, 1999, p. 315) captures the concern of many beginning social work students as they first approach group work assignments.

Experienced practitioners also have worries about group work, and it is not surprising that field instructors also voice trepidation as they begin to think about supervising students' group assignments. In one study, more than 80 field instructors were asked about their fantasies about students' group work assignments (Cohen, 1993). The diverse nature of the field instructors' responses in this study is striking, in that they represent a wide range of feelings about group work assignments. Some of their responses reflect fantasies of dramatic failure, as in the comment: "members will chew the leader up and spit her out." Less theatrical responses, such as: "members will not be willing to share," and the "worker will feel no connection to the group," also serve as barriers to launching new group assignments (p. 143). In sum, field instructors' concerns clustered around the following, often interrelated, themes:

- Worker will lose control of the group.
- Members will exhibit excessive hostility and act out.
- Members will be unmanageably resistant.
- Members will be overwhelmingly dependent on the worker.
- Group will disintegrate.
- Agency staff will judge the worker to be inadequate.

The overwhelming proportion of negatively phrased concerns indicates a large reservoir of field instructor fear about their own abilities and their students' performance with groups.

These findings are consistent with studies of other social work educators preparing students for social work practice with groups, including Shulman's (1999). He coined the term "fear of groups syndrome," and described it as a phenomenon common to most beginning workers. Kurland, Getzel, and Salmon (1986) suggest that students' and beginning workers' fears about starting groups should be considered normative, and question the common myth of the born group worker, who engages in group work practice with no trepidation. Even students with a natural gift for group work can have fears. Equally untrue is the part of the born group worker myth that implies that group work skills cannot be learned since they are inborn talents of a lucky few. In truth, skilled group work practice can be learned by nearly all social work students, given solid education, support, and experience. Believing otherwise legitimizes limiting exposure to group work, which in turn reinforces students' beliefs in their own inadequacies.

Facing Fears and Worries

In a profession that embraces the strengths perspective (Saleebey, 1998) it may seem odd to dwell on students' negative feelings about group work practice. However, it is important to remember that students' concerns can become self-fulfilling prophecies. In fact, field instructors who acknowledge students' feelings will find that the seeds of success are often imbedded in these fears of failure. Field instructors can use knowledge of potential fears as they prepare to introduce group assignments, and seek to create an environment in which students' feelings can be explored. Thus, while it remains important to reach for students' strengths and positive motivations, it is equally important to anticipate and encourage the expression of worries. As these concerns are expressed, students and field instructors can search for antidotes. Both field instructors and students will need to call upon their own awareness and use of self in this process. In being open to sharing concerns about working with clients in groups, the self-awareness of both partners will be strengthened.

Reassurances about working with groups can be found in students' own experiences. Reviewing with students why they wanted to become social workers can remind them of how they see themselves as people who feel positively about others. Some students may recall that they were considered good leaders or good listeners in previous group encounters. Others may remember enjoying the stimulation that accompanies some of the anxieties in group situations. Through the exploratory process, fears become reframed into "normal" worries about a new and important undertaking. In fact, fears can help some students to recognize the need for humility in the face of working with clients.

Balancing Hopes, Fears, and Regrets

The parallel process of student learning and client engagement can serve to help students take a look at their own "self in situation." Just as a client's motivation can be seen as a delicate balance between believing that something positive can happen and disappointment that it has not happened already (French, 1952), students can be helped to see that new challenges are normally met with a combination of hope, fear, and regret. We know that clients are motivated when they see that change will aid them in achieving goals to which they have significant commitment. Thus, field instructors should focus on students' passion for joining the profession, and the process of learning that makes their acculturation possible. In their landmark work on motivation, Ripple, Alexander, and Polemis (1964) found that workers' immediate attention to supporting and building on clients' hopes in initial sessions was the most important factor in engaging clients in effective problem solving. It would appear that the same strategy would be helpful with students. As social workers, we have the confidence to ask clients to face their fears and take leaps of faith to achieve their goals for change. Similarly, field instructors need to help students acknowledge ambivalence (and its universal nature) early in the supervisory process to enable them to take learning risks necessary to achieving their professional aspirations.

Seeing Fears as Signals

Another strategy for exploring students' feelings about groups is to find out whether they are specific to group work practice, or generalized to other areas as well. For example, it is quite possible that students' concerns about group assignments echo worries about their work with individuals, families, or communities. In such cases, field instructors may want to explore other concerns that students feel less comfortable expressing. For other students, concerns about group work mirror their usual feelings when approaching any unfamiliar situation (such as a new assignment). With these students, instructor sensitivity to the pace at which students enter practice will be important. A later section of this chapter, related to students' stages of development in field work, may be helpful in understanding student readiness and apprehensions.

Alternately, students may display fear about groups through telegraphed messages about the pace or content of supervision. For example, a student's worry that the group members will overwhelm her may correspond to a feeling that she is losing her sense of self in the field education process. Thus, field instructors must continually employ their listening skills, hearing both manifest and latent messages from students.

Drawing from Past Experiences with Groups

Student approaches to group work may be unique to the group modality, perhaps based on discomfort in social situations or on difficult encounters as group members. In these instances, field instructors need to walk a fine line between therapizing supervision, and helping students reflect on past experiences in order to move forward in professional practice. Again, starting where the student is is the best guide, as field instructors judge the ability of students to look back on these experiences. In most cases, reminiscing about feelings of vulnerability in groups will allow students to see what they learned in the past, help them identify with the possible concerns of group members, identify strategies for overcoming fears, and successfully engage in group work practice. For a very small number of students, significant traumas may ultimately prevent them from becoming effective group work practitioners. These students should be helped to find ways of participating and contributing to social work groups other than in leadership roles, as well as helped to identify additional arenas for their social work practice. If these important issues are not raised early in the field instruction process, they will compromise students' group work performance and continually reemerge until they are dealt with satisfactorily.

Learning about Group Work Practice

Students' fears about groups also stem from common misunderstandings about group dynamics and the role of the worker in social work practice with groups. Many fears are predicated on students thinking that they will be held wholly responsible for controlling the group experience. Worries about their authority become less potent as students assume facilitative, empowering roles which foster members' ownership and responsibility for their own group experience (Kurland & Salmon, 1998). Rather than worrying about losing control, students begin to see the group worker's role as helping the members assume control. As Miller (1987) states: "the worker must be willing to have less control over the helping process than in a one-to-one helping relationship" (p. 753). Thus, as they work with groups, most students will engage more in letting go of control than holding on to it.

Other students' initial concerns may stem from a misunderstanding of the group as a free for all, in which the worker has no accountability or authority. It takes experience with groups to understand the distinction between excessively controlling members' behaviors and responsibly assuming authority to help groups and members accomplish their goals. Students must be taught that as group workers, they retain their positions as guardians of a group's purpose and contract throughout the life of the group (Henry, 1992). While an integral part of the group, workers can never abandon their legitimate authority in order to become "one of the gang" (Kurland & Salmon, 1993).

Regardless of the source and dimensions of student fears, field instructors need not worry that discussing them in supervision will confirm spurious ideas about social work practice with groups. Rather, giving voice to the fears can validate students' constructive self-reflection and movement toward learning. Unexamined concerns can be damaging to future practice, as documented in Knight's (1997) study of students' attitudes toward group work. She found that students with group assignments, but without supervision, felt that they were less likely to work with groups after graduation than students without any group assignments in the field. Students who both worked with groups and had their group assignment supervised were those most likely to expect to work with groups in the future.

As stated by Lowy (1983), a productive supervisory relationship is one in which the learner feels that: "his or her ideas are genuinely respected and appreciated, even though they may not necessarily be valid, relevant, or correct" (p. 58). Such an open approach makes mistakes and errors permissible, and encourages creativity and risk-taking. The wide range of student concerns about working with groups indicates that discussion of these worries is warranted before and during student engagement with groups

Tuning in to Students' Perspectives on Practice with Groups

Tuning in is a strategy developed by Schwartz (1971), to help workers avoid self-fulfilling prophecies based on stereotypical views of clients. It is a form of "preliminary empathy," through which workers prepare themselves to receive client cues that can be difficult to detect with insensitive instruments (such as unprepared workers). The process is readily applicable to supervision of social work students in the field, and includes both affective and intellectual elements (Shulman, 1999). Tuning in provides the basis for a tentative contract with a student, suggesting ideas about pacing, assignments, and areas that might be explored in supervision.

Germain and Gitterman (1996) describe tuning in as a four-step process, including identification, incorporation, reverberation, and detachment. Although developed for workers preparing for clients, these steps (with the addition of a final step, openness), can guide field instructors preparing to supervise students in group work. Field instructors can use these steps as mental exercises, sensitizing them to what may be of concern to their students. Many field instructors have found it helpful to write down their thoughts during each step, to further examine what is by nature a private process.

Step One: Identification

In the first step, identification, field instructors attempt to glean what students are feeling and thinking as they approach work with groups. Operationally, field instructors should ask: *What do I know about this student's attitudes, experiences, and preparation for group work practice?* In answering, field instructors can rely on background information about a particular student, as well as knowledge about common experiences of beginning students. For example, field instructors generally know the age and previous social work experience of each student prior to field work. In addition, they may know the student's cultural background, social work experience, and practice interests. All of these are parameters that contribute to the assessment of each student.

Step Two: Incorporation

As part of the incorporation step, field instructors attempt to further understand students' feelings about groups by placing themselves in students' shoes. The operative question is: *If I were going through what this student is experiencing, how would I be feeling about working with groups?* During this stage, field instructors can freely imagine themselves in students' shoes, as long as they remember that they are learning about how they themselves feel in the shoes, not the way students feel when wearing them.

Field instructors have a special advantage as they engage in the incorporation process—they have been students themselves facing new challenges in the field. It is important for field instructors to catalogue their feelings at this step, even when the student's shoes pinch, or bring back uncomfortable recollections. In addition to helping to understand how an individual student may be feeling about groups, field instructors' reminiscences and projections at this stage will signal areas they will need to address within themselves to effectively supervise students. For example, when field instructors imagine the student to be highly anxious and resistant to group work assignments they may have guessed at a real student concern, brought their own worries to full consciousness, or both. The field instructor must work at separating these two.

Step Three: Reverberation

Reverberation is the step during which field instructors attempt to evoke their own life processes in order to facilitate understanding of students' experiences. Field instructors should ask themselves: *What analogous experience in my life can I use to imagine how the student is feeling at this time?* As already noted, field instructors should have no problem finding analogues for understanding. In addition to reflecting back on their own field work experiences, field instructors can try to stretch their thinking to other comparable situations with groups, such as working with staff teams, or entering a new group experience as a member.

Each sequential stage of this internal process yields insights into the ambiguities and subtleties of students' experiences, and field instructors may notice this step deepens their analysis. For example, in the identification stage, a field instructor might think of a particular student as anxious. In the incorporation stage, the vague term "anxious" is further elaborated and specified to include the student's possible worries about how group members will see them. This can create both excitement and fear of failure. Next, in the reverberation stage, the field instructor's own emotional experiences may suggest that the student's feelings are even more complex, including the possibility that the student may be carrying family members' expectations of him/her, at the same time as feeling liberated by learner status. Again, caution is warranted. Field instructors should avoid making the leap to thinking that their ideas about a particular student are actual facts. However, as imaginings, they can serve to open a field instructor up to the complexity of a student's experience.

Step Four: Detachment

In the fourth step, detachment, field instructors disengage themselves from the feelings that have been generated though the previous steps, and engage in rational, objective analysis of the data they have collected. This step must include conscious recognition that the ideas generated through the steps of incorporation and reverberation are all hypothetical and highly speculative. They are the result of field instructors mining their own experiences, rather than gathered through discussions with students.

Every thought collected through the process of detachment is considered data in trying to answer the question: *What might it all mean, and how can my findings inform the supervisory process?* At the least, field instructors are clued in to the possibility that they do not know everything about a particular student. In addition, they may have found a new entry point, suggesting that they explore a particular issue with a student, such as their previous experience with groups or their thinking about working in a particular setting.

Step Five: Openness

The first four steps in the tuning in process culminate in the fifth step of openness, in which field instructors develop an approach to meet students where they are, rather than where they are expected to be. Saying goodbye to the world of the imagination may be difficult— after all, it is so much more predictable than work with actual human beings. Nonetheless, field instructors must ask themselves: *How will I achieve the receptivity needed to develop effective plans with this student?* For some field instructors this task may entail working through some of the feelings brought up during the tuning in process so they do not interfere with the emerging relationship with the student. Field instructors may want to talk through the tuning in experience with peers to debrief the activity. For others, a brisk walk around the block (or some other way to clear one's head) may be the best way to achieve the openness necessary to be present to individual students as work in the real world resumes.

Field instructors can also adapt the tuning in process to help students understand group members. When students are guided through the steps, they are better able to grasp the range of members' feelings and concerns. Each step can bring a broader view, and while the data generated can be confusing and contradictory, it can help students view clients as multifaceted human beings. Tuning in can be particularly helpful in understanding common feelings of clients entering groups and for thinking about where the group as a whole may be going. The challenge in using this technique is the same whether it is practiced by students to understand group members or field instructors to understand students. Both field instructors and students need to be able to step away from their imaginings in order to be emotionally present, while at the same time using the ideas generated in the process as possible entry points for work in the group.

Stages of Learning Applied to Students' Practice with Groups

Social work students progress through stages of learning, albeit in a variable and fluid manner. They generally move from greater to lesser anxiety and from lesser to greater confidence and competence. Students may not go through all stages during a single field placement experience or during their social work education, since some may enter with solid experience, and leave with learning to be accomplished. With this in mind, it is to the advantage of field instructors to assess students' stages of learning when they enter and as they progress through supervision, in order to adjust supervisory strategies accordingly. Reynolds' (1942/1985) five distinct stages of student development, elaborated in the following sections, serve as a template for understanding student progress. These stages are further illustrated by reflections from students in the field.

Stage One: Acute Consciousness of Self

During the first stage, acute consciousness of self, students are immobilized by fear and confusion about their ability to intervene in the lives of others. This initial anxiety can act as both a stumbling block and a motivating force as students struggle to move forward. Adult students may find this stage particularly troubling, as they seek to balance their need for autonomy and self-direction with the dependency inherent in this stage of the learning process (Bogo, 1983).

This stage is characterized by intense and widespread worries about engaging in group work practice. One might wonder whether the fears contribute to the immobilization, or are artifacts of the acute self-involvement during this stage. Anyone who has suffered from stage fright is familiar with this phenomenon, in which neither one's body nor mind can be mobilized for constructive action. This phenomenon is analogous to Garland, Jones, and Kolodny's (1973) concept of each group member's self-consciousness, which they describe as part of the first stage of group development.

Fortunately, most students pass through this first stage quickly, when their desire to engage in the work overtakes their need for safety. Students in this stage push themselves to go forward. Field instructors need to provide the security for students to find their own footing amidst the uncertainty. However, when students languish in this first stage, field instructors must take another look at the immobilizing concerns, asking whether they are normative, or represent more serious issues for learning. In addition, field instructors need to ask themselves whether their own fears and fantasies about group work practice are contributing to students' anxieties.

Field instructors can engage students in planning for groups and tuning in to prospective members as a way to bring them into working with the group before the first meeting. Thus, the group assignment begins with the "pre-group phases" of developing an idea and proposal for the group, engaging others in the planning process, and beginning to convene potential group members (Hartford, 1971). Through this work, students are gently and systematically oriented to group work practice.

Stage Two: Sink-or-Swim Adaptation

The second stage of student learning, sink-or-swim adaptation, can be characterized by almost desperate, robotic activity. According to Reynolds (1942/1985):

> Like a poor swimmer falling into the water, he may have little sense of where the wharf is or how to get there, but he may succeed in keeping afloat at least, till he knows where he is and can save himself or be rescued. (p. 77)

This stage can last quite a while. During this stage students evidence a beginning grasp of group work principles, but without consistent application or ownership. Students may appear so completely devoted to getting it right and gaining the approval of the field instructor that they limit their ability to use themselves and their feelings effectively in service to the group. As the following student reflection indicates, this can be a painful, but valuable experience:

> I did a reminiscence group at a senior center in Brooklyn. The horrible thing was that I was very nervous when I just started doing this, and I had never done anything like this before. I

was over-prepared. I had written my notes over, and over, and over again. I had the whole thing planned out—and the thing was—that it just didn't go the way it was supposed to go. Plus, they didn't want to do reminiscence. I forgot, I wasn't listening to them—it was just the worst possible experience of my life. I am sure that you (my field instructor) must have felt that this person is going to have a long way to go, to figure out how she is going to work with this group of people.

And that was probably the beginning of everything—it was how you just don't know yourself. Well, I certainly wasn't trusting myself, and I thought I had to do everything and plan everything, and somehow everything would take care of itself. Each time, I had to come back the next week and in a way, start all over again. That was a very hard thing to do. The whole time they never really wanted to have a reminiscence group, and probably, if I had more confidence at the time, I would have changed the focus in the group and done something totally different—but I was intent on doing what I was supposed to—what I had set up to do.

This stage can also can be characterized by a "just do it!" philosophy that will vary with the type of learner. While some students benefit from this sense of abandon as an entry point to learning, others may end up believing that "doing it" without thought or sensitivity is enough. Therefore, at the same time that field instructors are urging beginning students to jump in without worrying so much, they must also establish the norm that unexamined practice is poor practice. The learning at this stage is in the struggle, and field instructors must help students engage in looking at their work. Field instructors may have to match students' concrete thinking during this stage by providing clear direction. Focusing on successful elements of students' interventions will help to build a fund of experience, increase self-confidence, and improve students' abilities to integrate classroom and field education as they move to advanced stages of learning.

Stage Three: Understanding the Situation without Power to Control One's Own Activity

As they move into the third stage of learning, that of understanding the situation without power to control one's own activity in it, students' capacity for insight increases and they are able to learn from reviewing their practice. Students demonstrate the ability to understand what should be done in a particular situation (usually too late to intervene effectively), but are not yet able to act on that knowledge on a consistent basis. Students present widely varying levels of skill, with uneven performance from week to week and from assignment to assignment.

In this stage, students begin to truly see groups as dynamic entities, and are able to separate what is happening in the group from their own preoccupations. However this stage, during which they are not able to consistently or reliably mobilize their new way of thinking into effective action, is perhaps the most difficult for students. Students' retreat to fears and blaming the group for difficulties in group functioning may signal their distress at knowing what to do without being able to master doing it. Field instructors will need to support students by identifying examples of partial success, and helping them appreciate the growth that is occurring. According to Reynolds (1942/1985), students can spend years in this stage; some never leave it.

Not surprisingly, students in their first year of group work field education have used the term "ordeal" to describe their experience (Barnat, 1973). The following recollection by a male student poignantly captures the essence of the third stage:

> This was the final group meeting of my 8th grade girls group at the local parochial school that took place in the front part of the office and Joan's (my field instructor) office was right behind the door. I had these seven girls in this meeting, and I'm not real great at termination. As a matter of fact I tend to just forget that I'm terminating with my clients. This was the last meeting, so this is when I was going to deal with termination and this story is kind of like how termination feelings can build up into a watershed and all of a sudden explode—and get way out of hand.

> I prepared myself for this, expecting that they might be acting out since it was the last group meeting. So all of a sudden, as I start to talk about this is the last meeting, they all start to speak in Spanish, and I don't speak Spanish. So, I am saying:"I'm wondering if this has anything to do with the last time we're meeting?"They didn't even, I wasn't even there, I wasn't even in the room, and I kept on trying that.

> I didn't know what to do. I kept saying, "this has got to have something to do with the last time we're meeting," and trying

to talk with them. They were speaking Spanish and they were saying all kind of curses in Spanish that I didn't know. And then I guess it all ended up that I just had nothing. I couldn't say anything, and then I tried to ask them to leave, but then I just broke down and started to cry—because I had lost control of the whole thing.

Actually, what was really nice was that Joan was right on the other side of the door listening to this whole thing and she came in and she dismissed the girls and we talked about it. But by then the girls wouldn't leave. Now they felt so guilty that they had made me cry. So it just got uglier and uglier. Then they were playing handball off the window at the front of the place— it was terrible—it was bad. So, that taught me something about preparing myself for termination, and also I might have been able to see a lot of these things building that I hadn't seen before, picking up latent content in the group work process that I wasn't so aware of—but that is about as bad as it has ever been.

This student's experience serves as a classic evidence of a learner in the midst of understanding the situation without power to control one's own activity in it. The vignette vividly portrays adolescent resistance to termination, and the student workers' inability to help the girls work through it to an effective ending. The intensity of feelings around termination contributes to the student's vulnerability around this issue, as well as his own hope to be further along as the field practicum was ending. Field instructors can imagine, or recall, the commitment to learning necessary to keep students engaged during this process, especially when it is preceded by the no less difficult stage of sink-or-swim adaptation. It is not uncommon for fears to reemerge at this stage, fueled by students' frustration at not being able to put their knowledge into consistent practice. Further, students can use these difficult experiences to confirm their fears and feelings of inadequacy. However, with the consistent support of field instructors and their growing ability to analyze group process, students are in a better position to examine these worries and advance their skills

When students cannot yet put their knowledge into practice, their self-awareness often becomes a topic for supervisory discussion. However, as Gitterman (1987) points out, self-awareness is necessary but insufficient in providing professional service: "The test is the extent to which it can be put into the service of helping others" (p. 25). Field instructors and students must remember to focus on the application of the student's self-awareness to work with the group. Students at this stage have a growing ability to develop plans for their work with the group, even if they are not fully realized. Through continual reflection back on the group and its members, students' self-awareness becomes a foundation for evaluating and building skills in group work.

Stage Four: Relative Mastery

Stage four involves the integration of students' personal and professional selves, enabling them to thoughtfully engage in the appropriate use of self with clients in groups. Gordon and Gordon (1982) describe this level as when students bring their personally constructed reality to the educational situation. Students at this stage have the capacity to honor previous life experiences, but are not held captive to the past. Social work students generally reach the stage of relative mastery by the end of graduate education, but field instructors should assess the level of students on an individual basis, evaluating their performance across levels and methods of practice.

Students often describe stage four as one of greater self-assurance and skill, and also as one of knowing how much is still to be learned. While some students report feeling less confident on graduation day than on the first day of school, others describe the transition to stage four as a feeling of not having to know the answer to everything. One student reflected:" I was just thinking, actually part of the struggle for me was just to accept that I am still in some ways just a beginner." Students in this stage identify the ongoing need for professional development and the ability to evaluate and adjust their own practice with clients, as well as bringing a new sense of perspective to their work, as in the following example:

> I had this group of sixth grade boys that were really out of control. . . They identified that they wanted to help themselves about being out of control and dealing with their anger, but it was one of the hardest—because the boys—they were sometimes fighting so much with each other or were acting out.

> We got through it, bit by bit, and at the end of the group I had them you know, talk a little about what they got out of it, and I expected them to like say: "Oh, I'm glad this is over," and a couple of them really had things to say. One of them who really was quite a liar, that was his way of getting through the world said:"well I learned that it's okay to lie—I can lie just a little bit of the time, but most of the time it's not okay to lie,"

and then he said that:"I learned to respect other people in this group, I learned to respect you" and for this kid, this was like something!

Supervision at this stage can feel more collegial, as students take increased responsibility for evaluating practice and planning interventions. They are now able to reliably and spontaneously adjust their performance in groups, and can take advantage of serendipitous moments with members. Through collaborative supervision, field instructors can help students find their own style of work, building on students' growing skills and self-awareness. Students are able to put their own fears and worries into a professional context, and can use their own learning process to tune in to clients' apprehensions and concerns in order to maximize the work of the group.

Stage Five: Learning to Teach What One Has Mastered

Students in field work may achieve relative mastery as well as demonstrate evidence of a beginning progression to stage five: "the stage of learning to teach what one has mastered" (Reynolds, 1942/1985, p. 83). Students' progress may be stronger in some areas than in others, and due to different educational paths, field instructors may find themselves working with students who have more finely tuned group work skills than they do. This should not be seen as a threat, but as an opportunity to engage in nonhierarchical, cooperative learning. Collaborative approaches to learning will move students forward at any stage, and is particularly important as the students' skills become more advanced. Students at this stage become less dogmatic, and more open to the strengths and skills of others. Sharing knowledge and skills is always important, but can become a dominant theme at this stage of learning, as the following story from a recent social work graduate working in a school setting demonstrates:

> A teacher was doing an intergenerational project. There was a conflict with a debating team about their schedule. The group had just started practicing, and she was trying to decide whether they were ready to debate in a meet. She thought there were pros and cons. If they didn't do it they would lose some experience, but if they did do it they might fail and then it might be a setback for them.
>
> She was trying to figure out all these crazy things and trying to decide for them about whether they were ready or not to do it and that was when I asked her: "Well, have you asked them

what they think about it? Let them have a discussion about it." She went back and did, and she was incredibly grateful. She thought I was the greatest on earth—brilliant!

Reynolds' fifth stage is generally reached after further experience in the field, as reported by the following student: "the way that I've changed is slowly, over time, relying less on my having to do everything, and relying more on the talent of the people around me." This stage is one of relative comfort with oneself as practitioner and as facilitator of another's learning and development. Of course, reaching this level does not mean never making a mistake in practice. Students struggling through field work are relieved to hear that mastery is not characterized by infallibility, but rather, the ability to make "more sophisticated mistakes," and more importantly, shortening the time between making errors and recognizing them (Shulman, 1999).

Most field instructors are in stage five. This stage is characterized by a release from the preoccupation with subject matter, accompanied by the ability to understand and respond to the particular challenges of the learner. Maintaining close ties to practice enables field instructors to directly experience the often illusive nature of competence. As a model for students, field instructors demonstrate the self-awareness, sense of perspective, and skill in using experience for learning that are the hallmarks of effective social work practice. Smalley's eloquent maxim about engagement with clients may be the best way to describe the joys and challenges of beginning field instructors as they enter a new learning cycle as social work educators: "Any beginning, any new understanding in life causes simultaneous feelings of hope and fear" (as cited in Fox, 1993, p. 1).

It seems natural that field instructors use their understanding about students' learning stages in their supervisory agenda. Students are participating in a parallel process, in which they differentially engage with the group, depending on the stage of the group's development. Similarities in supervision and group work practice exist, including the need for support and encouragement in the beginning stage, the increasing demand for work in the middle, and the responsibility for evaluation in the ending stage. Field instructors can build these parallels by asking their students to wonder about whether new group members feel something like the acute consciousness of self that they experienced as they began their first group assignment. Similarly, supervision can focus on how the student can facilitate opportunities for members to reflect on their struggles, and share their knowledge and experience in the group, since students have intimate knowledge of how this process can lead to growth.

Conclusion

This chapter presented a variety of strategies to help field instructors "start where the student is" in launching and supervising group work assignments. First, as part of the section on common fears, possible concerns of students were identified. This section continued with suggested themes for exploring these concerns.

The chapter proceeded with discussion of Schwartz's concept of tuning in, and its applicability to individualizing field instructors' approaches to work with social work students. Drawing from Bertha Reynolds' work (1942/1985), five stages were discussed as a useful frame of reference for differential supervision of students through the course of their internship.

Progression through these stages is not necessary linear, and students can appear to be at one stage in their work with groups, but in another in other methods of practice. However, field instructors will find that placing students' group work performance in the context of their stage of learning will broaden supervisory awareness and suggest a range of stage-appropriate interventions with students. For example, the common fears of "nobody talking" or "everybody talking" call for different teaching strategies depending on the students' stages of learning.

The assessment process requires that field instructors consider the unique and shared characteristics of each student approaching group work practice. Field instructors are charged with helping students access the best of themselves on clients' behalf. Part of the supervisory process is building students' self-awareness, and helping them move from knowledge into action. Through this exchange, students experience praxis, in which the cycle of understanding, action, and reflection becomes ongoing, leading to professional growth. Thus, "where the student is" becomes a place of growing confidence and competence.

References

Barnat, M. R., (1973). Student reactions to the first surprising year: Relationships and resolutions. *Journal of Education for Social Work, 9*(3), 3-8.

Bogo, M. (1983). Field instruction: Negotiating content and process. *The Clinical Supervisor, 1*(3), 3-12.

Cohen, C. S. (1993). Enhancing social group work opportunities in field work education (Doctoral Dissertation, Graduate School and University Center of the City University of New York, 1993). *Dissertation Abstracts International, 29*(3), 970.

Fox, R. (1993). *Elements of the helping process: A guide for clinicians.* Binghamton, NY: Haworth.

French, T. M. (1952). *The integrating behavior: Basic postulates.* Chicago: University of Chicago Press.

Garland, J. A., Jones, H. E., & Kolodny, R. L. (1973). A model for stages of development in social work groups. In S. Bernstein (Ed.), *Explorations in group work: Essays in theory and practice* (pp. 17-71). Boston: Milford House.

Germain, C., B., & Gitterman, A. (1996). *The life model of social work practice: Advances in theory and practice* (2nd ed.). New York: Columbia University Press.

Gitterman, A. (1987). Field instruction in social work education: Issues, tasks and skills. *Jewish Social Work Forum, 23,* 24-27.

Goldstein, H. (1983). Starting where the client is. *Social Casework, 65*(5), 267-275.

Gordon, W. E., & Gordon, M. S. (1982). The role of frames of reference in field instruction. In B. W. Sheafor & L. E. Jenkins (Eds.), *Quality field instruction in social work* (pp. 21-36). New York: Longman.

Hartford, M. E. (1971). *Groups in social work: Application of small group theory and research to social work practice.* New York: Columbia University Press.

Henry, S. (1992). *Group skills in social work: A four-dimensional approach* (2nd ed.). Pacific Grove, CA.: Brooks/Cole.

Knight, C. (1997). A study of MSW and BSW students' involvement with group work in the field practicum. *Social work with Groups, 20*(2), 31-49.

Kurland, R., Getzel, G., & Salmon, R. (1986). Sowing groups in infertile fields: Curriculum and other strategies to overcome resistance to the formation of new groups. In M. Parnes (Ed.), *Proceedings of the annual group work symposium. Innovations in social group work: Feedback from practice to theory* (pp. 57-74). Binghamton, NY: Haworth.

Kurland, R., & Salmon, R. (1993). Not one of the gang: Group workers and their role as an authority. *Social Work with Groups, 16*(2), 153-169.

Kurland, R., & Salmon, R. (1998). *Teaching a methods course in social work with groups.* Alexandria, VA: Council on Social Work Education.

Lowy, L. (1983). Social work supervision: From models toward theory. *Journal of Education for Social Work, 19*(2), 55-62.

Miller, I. (1987). Supervision. In Anne Minahan (Ed.-in-Chief), *Encyclopedia of social work* (18th ed., pp. 748-756). New York: NASW Press.

Reynolds, B. (1985). *Learning and teaching in the practice of social work.* Silver Spring, MD: National Association of Social Workers. (Original work published 1942)

Ripple, L., Alexander, E., & Polemis, B. (1964). *Motivation, capacity and opportunity: Studies in casework theory and practice.* Chicago: School of Social Service Administration, University of Chicago.

Saleebey, D. (1998). *The strengths perspective in social work practice* (2nd ed.). New York: Longman.

Schwartz, W. (1971). On the use of groups in social work practice. In W. Schwartz & S. R. Zalba (Eds.), *The practice of group work* (pp. 3-24). New York: Columbia University Press.

Shulman, L. (1999). *The skills of helping individuals, families, groups and communities* (4th ed.). Itasca, IL: F.E. Peacock.

Chapter 7 | Planning Group Work Assignments

Pre-group planning is recognized as a vital component of social work practice with groups (Glassman & Kates, 1990; Henry, 1992; Kurland, 1978; Steinberg, 1997; Toseland & Rivas, 2001). However, it also appears that social work students and practitioners give inconsistent (and sometime nonexistent) attention to planning in their work (Cohen, 1995; Knight, 1993; Wayne & Garland, 1990). In this seemingly contradictory reality lays the planning paradox, making the planning of groups one of the most important and least practiced aspects of social work.

Field instructors are in an ideal position to put this paradox to rest by encouraging students to build the necessary skills for effective planning of their group work practice. Although building on generalist concepts, planning group assignments requires specialized knowledge of how to work simultaneously with multiple clients, and how to foster relationships among them as a vehicle for goal achievement.

This chapter begins by exploring some of the reasons for the planning paradox, followed by the description and application of a model for planning group work assignments. The chapter concludes with a worksheet for planning, and a sample completed worksheet that is used to suggest the variety and options in planning students' assignments.

Challenges in Effective Planning of Groups

It is important to identify, understand, and address the forces that may inhibit effective planning for group work assignments in field education. This section addresses three challenges: defining pre-group planning, working in a professional context with groups, and maximizing client self-determination.

Defining Pre-group Planning

It is possible that the wide range of ideas about what constitutes a plan creates confusion about how to proceed with students in field education. Synonyms of the word plan include sketch, design, scheme, or plot. The American Heritage Dictionary (Pickett, 2000) of the English Language's citation for a plan includes the following definitions:

1. A scheme, program, or method worked out beforehand for the accomplishment of an objective; a plan of attack.

2. A proposed or tentative project or course of action.

3. A systematic arrangement of important parts: a configuration or outline.

4. A drawing or diagram made to scale showing the structure or arrangement of something. (p.1341)

This dictionary citation provides a useful overview of what comprises a solid plan for a social work group. Indeed, an effective plan should include elements of each of these definitions.

The notion of working out the plan beforehand is included in the first definition. While this may sound obvious, it is vital that a plan be developed before the process of group formation begins. The second definition highlights the tentative nature of a plan. One of the most useful pieces of advice for students is: "over plan and under use," since it captures the importance of developing an extensive plan, and then being prepared to move in the direction of the group, even when it diverges from the original design. In other words, group workers must be prepared to go from "Plan A" to "Plan B," and so on, as the group forges its own identity and sense of common purpose. The third definition reinforces the metaphor of a plan as a sketch or outline, reminding us that it is not a fully drawn script, but a roughly drawn framework that includes key elements. The final definition suggests that a plan provides a representation of these key elements and elaborates on their interrelationship.

Working in a Professional Context with Groups

Students may notice that attention to planning differs within an agency, depending on system size (e.g., work with individuals is planned more thoroughly than group work), on client population (e.g., work with adults is planned more thoroughly than with children), or on other dimensions such as fees or regulations attached to particular services. Professional social work practice with groups and other systems requires knowledge of organizational assessment and intervention which calls for social workers to become "conscious contrarians" (Mondros & Wilson, 1994), who will push for critical examination of agency practices and policies. Through critical examination, students learn how to be responsible professionals rather than technicians who thoughtlessly carry out agency mandates and perpetuate dysfunctional patterns regarding group work practice. Insufficient or incomplete planning is one such pattern.

From a professional social work perspective, engaging in thoughtful planning is an ethical imperative (Lewis, 1982), part of our commitment to providing quality services to clients. However, this ethical imperative has been applied to work with groups differently than to other forms of intervention (Garland, 1992). It is unfortunate that in many agencies, planning a group is given the same or even less attention than preparing a guest list for a dinner party. Such inattentive planning is supported by the belief that only intuitive, common social skills are needed to develop group services. However, planning of groups should be approached with the same professional rigor as other interventions. It requires both generalist practice skills and familiarity with specialized knowledge regarding group dynamics and stages of development. Planning group assignments builds on existing knowledge, but requires acquisition of new skills and perspectives.

Maximizing Client Self-determination

Another challenge to effective planning is the belief that pre-group planning by workers limits self-determination of members. Reasoning that the members should be the ones to develop the group's design, workers might dismiss calls for preliminary planning as paternalistic. At first blush, this view has some validity. After all, what should the worker's role be in developing what is essentially the members' group? What stops planning from being deterministic and manipulative?

It is true that we are obligated to maximize clients' rights to self-determination to the extent possible (National Association of Social Workers, 1996). Yet in practice with groups, workers must consider the rights of individual members within the context of the group as a whole, which has collective purpose and rights. Therefore, it is essential that workers begin the process of group formation with a tentative purpose in mind, even if this precludes some possibilities for the group. Without this initial proposal, members cannot be recruited in good faith. In effect, the clear statement of initial purpose allows members to maximize their self-determination in deciding whether to become a part of the group, and helps members to understand that the rights of the collective is sometimes more important than individual self-determination (Falck, 1988).

Group workers abdicate their responsibility if they pretend that clients can do whatever they wish (Bernstein, 1993; Kurland & Salmon, 1992). Rather, as professionals, we are obligated to engage in pre-group planning in order to protect members' rights and assume our legitimate authority (Kurland & Salmon, 1993). In fact, refusal to plan effectively is analogous to withholding the service that clients have a right to expect—access to the workers' expertise. As Konopka (1997) states: "The group worker is a person who is not better than the members, but has, hopefully, a bit more knowledge about, and insight into, group life and functioning" (p. 4).

Reframing ideas about planning is needed to move from a view of planning as conspiring to a view of planning as proposing. In the first analogy, planning is a sinister activity, with the worker seen as a schemer and manipulator of clients. In the second analogy, planning is a service that the worker contributes to the relationship, presenting a draft to begin the process of member deliberation. The model of planning as proposing capitalizes on the worker's strength as an agency insider and professional, who brings knowledge of the service environment and of social group work practice to the members. As a consultant, the worker is not presumed to hold the answers to clients' problems, but uses skills to foster collaborations through which solutions can be found (Gutierrez, 1990). In this way, planning is not imperialistic, but focused on empowerment and extending the limits of self-determination.

Using a Model for Pre-group Planning

Drawing from the preceding discussion, a useful model for pre-group planning should have the following characteristics:

- Adaptable to a variety of agency environments
- Promotes member participation in determining the group's direction
- Useful to prepare for group inauguration
- Provides guidelines that can be used flexibly
- Includes critical elements of group life
- Diagrams the relationship of elements to each other

Kurland's (1978) landmark work on pre-group planning provides such a model. In addition to identifying key areas for attention during the planning process, the model depicts elements in relation to each other, suggesting a sequence for their consideration. Figure 1 is based on Kurland's planning model for when the group's composition is not predetermined. As the figure illustrates, the approach to planning discussed in the following pages has the following eight components: Agency and social context, Need, Purpose, Composition, Structure, Content, Formation strategy, and Evaluation. Each component will be discussed separately, although it should not be inferred that they should (or can) be considered in isolation. In fact, they overlap.

Agency and Social Context

As illustrated in the model, agency and social context serve as the outside sphere for the group, providing the environment and boundary. This sphere includes factors and influences from the agency and larger environment that might affect the worker, clients, and the group being formed (Kurland & Salmon, 1998). These parameters serve to focus attention on possible group assignments for students in this environment, and steps necessary to insure agency sanction and staff cooperation.

Once the idea for the group takes shape, social workers, (including field instructors and students) bring special knowledge of the organizational and community setting to the potential group members. In a sense, they will be acting as ambassadors of the agency to the members and also as ambassadors of the members to the agency. As group planners, students should keep field instructors and other staff informed about the ongoing work of the group, and complete the cycle by feeding information back to group members. They will need to consider the multiple dimensions that contribute to the groups' success. Even the most mundane details can be critical, as Reid (1996) recalls: "Many groups have stood on the steps of an agency while a worker frantically searched for someone to unlock the door because the worker forgot to inform the maintenance staff that there would be an evening meeting" (p. 187). Also important is the reevaluation of the impact of the agency and social environment on the group as the plan takes shape. As each element of the plan is added, new insights may be revealed that will facilitate group formation.

The plan for the Grandmothers as Mother's Again support group contained in this chapter's Appendix B, provides an example of how the agency and social environment affect the development of a group assignment. Preceding the group's formation, the field instructor, student, and agency administrators had been looking for a group assignment for the student. Through this search, they concluded that from

Figure 1

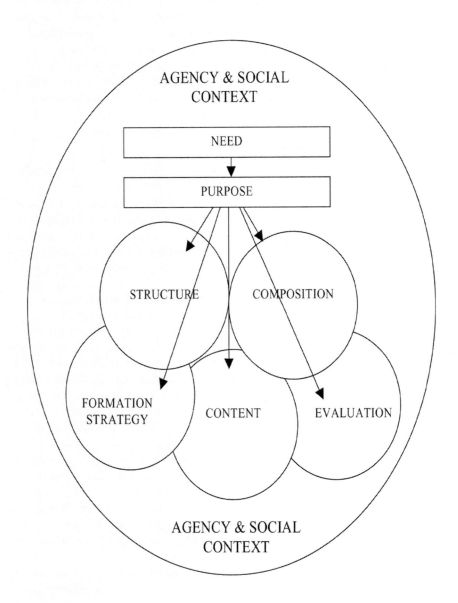

the agency's point of view, three conditions were necessary: the group had to be a new initiative since the existing groups were not appropriate assignments; it had to serve real and important needs; and it had to be sustainable beyond the student's placement. Serendipitously, three grandmothers in the community approached a staff member with the words: "Son, this is important!" and went on to describe their need to meet and help each other with the challenge of raising grandchildren (Cohen, 1995).

As the planners explored the request further, they discovered that the local community was highly supportive of the proposed program, and many neighborhood organizations were eager to publicize the group. A local church and a settlement house even offered meeting space to make the site convenient for potential members. The idea for the group survived a lengthy start-up period because it met the conditions set by the agency. The group was integral to the agency mission and had the potential for positive benefits to clients and the program. It was well within the boundaries of the agency and social context, and capitalized on the support within those venues.

It should be noted that the particular design of the group was not the only choice available, nor was it the only *good* idea. For example, the agency could have convened the original delegation of grandmothers with representatives of local organizations interested in the problem of second-time grandparents; a resulting task force could have developed a program or built on an existing service. Such a committee also would have served as a legitimate group assignment for the student. Other group assignments could have been generated through analysis of the variety of agency and social environments. These might have included a peer support group for leaders of grandparent-focused programs, an advocacy training group for grandparents seeking permanent custody, or a kinship care group of grandmothers engaged in the child welfare system (Cohen & Pyle, 2000).

Need

In an ideal situation, field instructors and students would begin this step in the planning process by considering the variety of wants, drives, problems, issues, or areas of concern that exist among those in the agency's target populations. However, such a broad-based inquiry is rare in today's service environment. Rather, most potential group assignments have taken some shape before the planning process, and may begin to be defined by a structural element (e.g., a group to meet on Thursday afternoons), a content element (e.g., art group), or a pur-

pose (e.g., preparing for parenthood). Alternately, an initial need assessment may suggest naturally occurring groups (including staff teams)
as potential assignments. In other words, planning does not always
begin at the beginning or the logical starting point; group planning
often begins with the givens of agency or client situations.

Needs are considered in relation to specific clients rather than in
relation to an overall population in situations where the group's membership is known at the onset of planning. These cases might include
particular residents of group home, clients drawn from existing
caseloads, or a cohort of patients completing treatment. Students may
also encounter the situation where membership is known at the onset
if they step into an assignment previously carried by a former intern.
In other cases, a group is found already formed with an existing membership, as in the case of natural groups. Whether the process of composition is wide open or begins with selecting individuals or the group
as a whole, planners will need to identify a client population to be
served, and the anticipated needs of that population. Even when the
membership is known at the onset of planning, it remains important
to consider member needs before further defining purpose, and subsequently structure, content, formation, and evaluation strategies.

In the example of the grandmothers' group, the planners considered the possible needs of grandparents suddenly confronted with
full-time responsibility for their grandchildren. Needs were thought to
be financial (e.g., new expenses, job demands), physical (e.g., difficulty in taking on new activities, exhaustion) social (e.g., isolation from
peers and former activities), informational (e.g., understanding child
welfare and educational systems) and emotional concerns (e.g., feelings of failure and inadequacy). While the primary needs addressed by
the group were expected to be support and education, other needs
surfaced during this stage of planning and entered into the group's
life through discussion and mutual aid by the membership.

Purpose

Since a single group cannot address all of the needs of a potential
membership, the next step in planning is to tentatively identify the
purpose that members will collectively pursue. Each individual member must find the proposed purpose important enough to invest their
energy and overcome the risks to involvement. It may be useful to use
the person-in-environment framework as a point of reference. With
this framework, possible group purposes can be formulated that
focus on:

- The person, helping members address individual needs they share (e.g., support group)

- The environment, helping members make changes in the larger system (e.g., staff committee)

- The interaction of person and environment, helping members negotiate the interface between themselves and systems (e.g., re-entry group)

It should be noted that these types of distinctions (as elaborated in chapter 4) are developed to bring clarity to the assignment's purpose; they are not meant to be mutually exclusive.

Once a clear statement of purpose is proposed and can be articulated by students, they can move on to developing the other five elements of the group. For the group described in the appendix, the statement of purpose was "to help grandmothers feel supported and more able to cope with raising their grandchildren." As a statement of purpose this was clear, flowed from the needs assessment, and was within the function of the agency to serve vulnerable populations (Cohen, 1995). A statement of group purpose should include reference to desired outcomes. Such a broad statement of purpose sets the stage for evaluation of group success. Students working with groups should be prepared to share the proposed statement of purpose at the first meeting, and in pre-group contacts with potential members. Worries that they will not be able to state it directly to the members may signal that the purpose is either unclear or inappropriate. Students' concerns may also indicate their resistance or inadequate understanding of the contacting process with clients in groups.

Unlike their predecessors, the remaining elements (composition, structure, content, formation strategy, and evaluation) are not sequential. While it is impossible to think about all of them simultaneously, it will be important to consider how one affects the other. Achieving harmony among the elements requires review and readjustment. Workers must continually look back to insure that the five elements support the accomplishment of the group's purpose and meet members' needs, while being in concert with the agency and social environment.

Composition

According to Olmstead's (1959) definition, a group is:

A plurality of individuals who are in contact with one another, who take one another into account, and who are aware of some

> significant commonality—an essential feature of a group is that
> its members have something in common and that they believe
> that what they have in common makes a difference. (p. 21)

It is the nature of this "significant commonality" that must be considered in balancing the levels of heterogeneity and homogeneity in the group. Groups can tolerate a high level of diversity when what they share in common is experienced intensely, such the experience of being recently widowed. In contrast, groups that are organized for more general purposes, such as learning to be better parents, may find that their diversity can divide, rather than enliven their work (Gitterman, 1989).

Paradise and Daniels (1973) point out that workers should strive for "balance," rather than "sameness" of members' characteristics during the process of group composition. Their definition of a balanced group, "one in which tensions and differences exist so that movement and action may take place" (p. 41), suggests that differences must exist. In fact, they see an unbalanced group as one in which there is too much sameness, or an overload of similarities in any one direction. While descriptive attributes of members (including demographic classifications) and behavioral attributes (including ways of acting with others) should be considered in composing groups, Bertcher and Maple (1974) suggest that behavioral attributes are more important, since they indicate how a prospective member will interact with others.

Differences add excitement, but solitary outliers (either in members or their characteristics) can confound group cohesion. Invoking the "sore thumb concept," Paradise and Daniels (1973, p. 42) suggest that "one of anything" creates an imbalance in the group's composition and suggest the following sets of continua for seeking a dynamic balance for the group:

- Passive–Aggressive
- Highly Skilled–Unskilled
- Other-Oriented–Self-Oriented
- Likeable–Difficult to Like
- Poor Reality Testing–Good Reality Testing
- Suggestive–Resistant to Suggestion

In essence, thoughtful composition maximizes members' opportunities to build positive relationships, a force seen as "enabling dynamism in the support, nurture, and freeing of people's energies and motivations toward problem solving and the use of help" (Perlman, 1979, p. 2).

In the case of the grandparent support group, it was decided to limit participants to women, since gender appears to be a key factor in establishing commonality (Cohen, 1997). Age was not considered a screen for membership, as long as grandmothers had custody (not necessarily legal) of their grandchildren or great grandchildren. Language was an issue considered by the planners, who decided that all potential members should be able to speak in English. The agency later inaugurated an exclusively Spanish-speaking group. Bilingual groups can be effective, but the workers were not prepared to take on that additional challenge. In this case, it was up to the field instructor and student to propose a group composition strategy that balanced issues of heterogeneity and homogeneity among members. Assigning primary planning responsibility to field instructors and students does not preclude modifying plans over time, or the inclusion of other participants in the planning process such as clients, potential members, and staff who have worked with similar groups.

Relationships can be fostered or stymied depending on the interaction of compositional factors with the other elements of the plan. Coming to a tentative decision about the size of the group is a good example of how these elements can interact. For example, the content of the Grandmothers' as Mothers Again support group outlined in appendix B was projected to be primarily discussion, suggesting a small group of 5–15 members. With the same purpose, but different content, the number of members selected might vary considerably. A social-action-focused group, advocating for reform of grandparent custody regulations, could include many more members, while an executive committee acting for a larger body could be significantly smaller and still be effective. A guiding principle in developing group assignments is to continually refer back to the purpose, and consider the synergistic effect of all elements of the plan in setting the stage for its fulfillment.

Group composition also includes the worker or workers. As discussed in chapter 5, making the choice of solo or co-leadership involves consideration of multiple variables. In the grandparent support group example, a co-leadership arrangement of a student and staff social worker was selected to best meet the agency's and members' needs as the group was inaugurated. Through supervisory conferences with both workers, the field instructor helped them develop a plan for their work together. In addition to combined supervisory sessions with the field instructor, the co-leaders met before and after every group meeting to plan and review their progress. The workers were encouraged to identify their own sense of connection with the group, and to use this self-awareness in their work. That they each had spent a great deal of time in the care of their own grandmothers deepened their connection to each other and to the members.

Structure

Structure as a noun can be thought of as the anatomy of the group; as a verb it can be seen as the process of creating a group identity (Middleman & Goldberg, 1972). The structure serves to identify roles for workers and members, provide behavioral expectations and sanctions, and through the group's work together, define a unique constellation of norms and rules to serve their purpose.

Formulating a tentative structure for the group is a complicated affair, including consideration about the following areas of group life:

- Meeting place, time, duration, frequency, and life-span
- Points of entrance and exit from the group
- Member-to-member and worker-to-member relationships outside the group
- Norms, rules, and decision-making practices
- Member and worker roles and responsibilities
- Member fees and costs of group operation
- Ancillary and collateral activities
- Agreements regarding confidentiality and management of information
- Degree of prescribed member roles or order of meeting content

Through the planning process, invisible structures can become visible, making the group's framework open to discussion and innovation. Thinking broadly during planning enriches the group's options, and can build students' repertoires of ideas for future group work practice.

As already noted, some of the decisions about group structure will be made before this stage of planning. For example, at one agency, groups may only meet in the evening; at another, fees may be charged for all client services, including membership in groups. Within this diversity of approaches is only one inviolable rule for planners: A group's structure must help the members accomplish the group's purpose. Thus, the temporal arrangements of the group should be designed to facilitate mutual aid among members (Gitterman, 1989), with structure following function (Magen, 1998).

While most structural arrangements must be dealt with early in the planning process (such as the time and frequency of meetings), others, such as decisions about confidentiality and the management of information are often overlooked. Yet, it is at the very onset of the group that participants must consider their right to privacy, their responsibility to other members, and the regulation of these decisions by outside forces (Cohen & Phillips, 1995). Planners need to consider which of these structural elements are mandated by agencies (e.g., record keeping and policies for sharing information with others) and which elements will need to be determined with the members (e.g., confidentiality among participants).

In the case of the support group for grandmothers, some of the structural arrangements were based on agency preferences (e.g., place, frequency, fees), some were selected after pre-group consultation with potential members (e.g., meeting time, when members can enter and exit the group), and some elements were left open for group members to take on once they began meeting (e.g., decision-making practices, confidentiality agreements). Some structural arrangements took longer to emerge and underwent revision during the life of the group like collateral activities between members and workers, and patterns of external relationships among members. Workers and other agency staff maintained their availability for information and referral services throughout the life of the group.

It is critical to leave open the possibility for structural change in the group as it evolves. For example, weekly or monthly meetings might suit the member's needs better than the biweekly arrangement developed when the group was first in the planning stage. Similarly, while the grandmothers' group did not ultimately find it necessary to develop a child-care component, other groups might see this as necessary to group success. A key lesson for students engaged in planning is to help them see which choices are open and available to the members for decision making, and which choices are made outside the group. Further, the worker has to plan to sensitively convey these distinctions to group members and invite their feedback.

Content

Group content or program refers to anything that takes place during the course of a meeting, whether it is making art, playing games, or having a discussion. Planning group content must focus on what the members will do to achieve their agreed-upon purpose (Kurland & Salmon, 1998). Thus, while the planning of group content identifies *what* the group will do, it is not divorced from thinking about *why* the group is engaging in a particular activity. As noted over fifty years ago by Grace Coyle (1948), a challenge for group planners is to maintain a focus on the group purpose and members, while planning for the content of the group:

> Success from the group worker's point of view is seen not in terms of games won, ceramics produced, or information learned, but in terms of what the experience means to the participants. (p. 28)

Maintaining this distinction is not always easy, since as noted in chapter 4, activity or content—such as singing or sports—identifies some groups. Helping students remember that activities are selected to accomplish group purposes will guard against displacement, in which the activity can become an end in itself.

Verbal and nonverbal strategies can be further categorized into dimensions of time (present, past, or future) and place (within the group experience or outside the group experience). To illustrate, the activity of talking can be broken down to focus on:

- Immediate, jointly held concerns of the members about themselves (e.g., entering into new relationships or self-care afterdischarge)

- Immediate, external, but common concerns (e.g., concerns about youth activities or inadequate heat in a building)

- Non-immediate, past-, future-, or fantasy-oriented concerns (e.g., reminiscence or imagining life on another planet)

The planners of the grandmother's support group described in appendix B developed a range of activities and content elements before the group began, and then added new elements with the members' input as the group became established. They anticipated the need for some opening activities, such as warm-ups that would help the members get to know each other, and strengthen their engagement with the group. These included exercises in which members reflected back to their own childhoods, and playfully recalled how they felt at ages corresponding to those of their grandchildren. After a few meetings, a check-in ritual was developed with the members, consisting of each member briefly sharing something that had happened since the last meeting. At the suggestion of the members, a closing ritual, including a prayer for families was developed, which sometimes incorporated affirmations by members regarding their plans and hopes for the coming weeks. Members suggested areas in which they would like further information, and speakers were periodically invited to bring material to the group. Discussions also led to collaborations between nearby grandparent support groups and with other service providers that engaged members in social action, recreation, and educational activities.

The group's planners learned an important lesson about the' importance of engaging the members in decision making about activities for the group. Before the group began, the planners thought that the members would be interested in joint activities with their grandchildren to address feelings of isolation. However, when workers suggested that the members plan such an outing, they found members particularly unenthusiastic. The group ultimately came to the conclusion that although an intergenerational event had some merit, the members cherished the group because it was just for them—a time away from their grandchildren. If the workers had not been open and ready to discuss these issues (even though they were highly invested in the idea of an intergenerational activity), the group would have been derailed from its purpose as members had came to define it.

This experience highlights the importance of students' learning to engage members in deciding the content of the group. Planners should first ask themselves the question: "Which medium of exchange will the members choose in attempting to meet their common needs?" (Shulman, 1971, p. 225) and should then push on and ask the members such questions throughout the life of the group. The key skill in the use of program planning is the worker's ability to understand and operationalize links between what the group does and how and why it does it.

Formation Strategy

This element of the planning process includes two key areas for deliberation: group formation and potential member orientation. First, in developing a formation strategy, the planners must consider what options will secure appropriate members for the group. Among possible strategies for group formation are the following:

- Referrals from other staff and professionals
- Selection of members from one's own caseload
- Assignment of members (mandatory participation)

- Announcement of the group and providing opportunities for members to volunteer
- Direct outreach to potential members
- Direct outreach to existing/natural groups

As already noted, preconditions to the composition process must be acknowledged. For example, the agency may restrict group participation to present clients, suggesting a recruitment strategy limited to clients on current caseloads. In such settings, colleagues could be solicited for referrals with a well-constructed prospectus for the group (Glassman & Kates, 1988). When membership recruitment requires direct pre-group contact with referral sources, planners should assess what they know and what they can assume about people (within and outside the agency setting) who are being asked to refer others to the group. These people, so essential to the formation process, may have reservations that need to be acknowledged and addressed. It can be expected that before referring potential members, they will need to believe in the benefits of the service being offered and have confidence in the professionals involved. Some referral sources will have concerns about sharing their clients with another professional, and students must be prepared to explore this and other areas in a competent manner if they hope to be provided with links to potential members.

In addition, students can be engaged in thinking about whether they should recruit members among clients they have been assigned to work with individually. Such a discussion can be a rich learning opportunity in supervision, as students consider the potential benefits and challenges of group participation for their clients, and the complexity of handling their own dual roles as case worker or group worker with the same client.

Recruitment may be as simple as publicizing the group and waiting for applicants to appear, or developing another type of strategy. Self-referrals are most likely when the issue to be addressed by the group is perceived as "normal," such as how to deal with rebellious adolescents, or how to cope with sibling rivalry. This approach to recruitment also requires potential members to have strong motivation for help and to change some behavior. On the other hand, announcements will rarely yield results if the issue to be addressed is one that causes embarrassment or shame, and potential members fear exposure. A student once reported putting up announcements of a group for battered women in the supermarket and other community settings, and was disappointed when no women showed up for the meeting.

This student had overlooked the lengths to which most women with this problem go to hide it from others.

Part of the identification of potential members is the challenge to motivate those appropriate for the group under consideration to participate. Sometimes this motivation comes from engaging with members around their strengths and interests, or from exploring the consequences of not participating. Potential members are likely to be interested in the other participants, the pressures for participation and limits of self-determination, and most importantly, what they can expect to gain from the experience.

A reading of Tropp (1971) suggests that all members enter new group experiences with the following questions:

- What is it all about?
- Who will be in it with me?
- What will the leader be like?

As compelling as these questions are, pre-group meetings are not always the best strategy for answering them. Rather, planners must examine whether members' feelings of uncertainty are obstacles to them coming to the first meeting, or common concerns that are best addressed at an initial meeting. Field instructors can help focus students' attention on the possible need to have a head start by meeting clients individually before a first meeting. Through such discussions, students learn that the decision to hold pre-group meetings should be made primarily on the basis of member (not worker or agency) needs.

Pre-group contacts should be considered when the idea for the group may be threatening or confusing to potential members. In many instances, students may need to meet with potential members to help them work through factors that may hold them back from wanting to join. Such meetings provide the opportunity to inquire about past group experiences that may affect their engagement, and are particularly advisable in situations where potential members must meet particular criteria.

In the case of the grandmother's support group, pre-group meetings were held on the telephone or in person to determine whether applicants met the membership criteria, as well as to orient potential members to the group's purpose, gather information about child-raising responsibilities, and to discover the best possible day and time for the meeting. It was important to recognize that by talking with applicants before the first meeting, the workers began the contracting and relationship-building process. They were encouraged to draw on their knowledge of these processes in order to clearly present their own roles, the nature of the agency, and the expectations of members. When students decide to meet with potential members before the first meeting, they must also consider the consequence of establishing tentative bonds between workers and individual members before the members meet each other at the first meeting.

An often overlooked strategy for group formation is to find a group that already exists. Social group work has its roots in working with natural groups, and the profession's movement towards a medical model has resulted in doing so less frequently. Students should be helped to recognize when this approach may be the most effective one. For example, the Grandmother's as Mother's Again program was initiated when a small group of friends approached the sponsoring agency for assistance. Other types of natural groups include those composed of:

- People that gather at the same time (e.g., parents picking up their children at a day care center each evening)

- People that gather in the same place (e.g., patients or family members in a waiting room)

- People that gather to engage in the same activity (e.g., teenagers playing basketball)

When forming the group in this manner, workers make initial overtures to the group as a whole, rather than to individual potential members. Students should be prepared for the special challenges of meeting clients "where they are" rather than one by one on the workers' home turf, the agency environment.

Regardless of their route to group membership, the effect of potential members' "degree of choice" about their involvement, and their path to the group will need to be identified (Germain & Gitterman, 1996). Once these conditions are understood, planners should focus on how the group's formation strategy will help members work together to meet their needs.

Evaluation

While it may seem unusual to develop evaluation strategies before a group begins meeting, accountability to agencies and clients' demands such an approach. For students, the evaluation component is essential in helping them understand what is happening, what they can learn from the group, and how to adjust their interventions. The Council on

Social Work Education (1994) has emphasized practice-based research and outcome assessment in social work education, including in group work practice. Field instructors may have encountered increased pressure to expand students' exposure and participation in research activities, including evaluation of their work with clients.

An evaluation strategy developed during the planning process must include the following components:

- Methods for monitoring the implementation of the plan
- Methods for documenting the process of the group
- Methods for assessing the achievement of group and individual outcomes

As discussed further in Chapter 8, a variety of evaluation strategies are available for consideration. As with the development of other elements, planners will need to consider the impact of decisions already made about the group's operation, and how to maximize the participation of members in selecting evaluation strategies.

The example of the grandparent support group demonstrates that an evaluation plan has both monitoring and assessment components. The workers' activity reports, process recordings and summary recordings individually captured key moments in the group's life, and collectively, its rich history. Supervisory conference agendas also served as evaluative tools when used to identify patterns and track key issues over time. In order to assess the accomplishment of the group's purpose, the planners proposed to discuss evaluation with the grandmothers. First, they acknowledged that the members and workers shared the concern that the group meet their needs. Second, they stated that they wanted to insure that the group took the form members were promised, and third, that they wished to monitor the group's progress with member input. Following discussion, the workers prepared to suggest a variety of assessment techniques, including using existing and group-generated measures, with the understanding that the members would have a primary voice in deciding which strategy was implemented. In the initial contracting stage, the members agreed to periodically review their expectations and experience of the group, and to reflect on whether (and how) the group was meeting their needs. As they moved further into the group, members used this information to review the group's purpose and revise its structure and content to support its accomplishment.

The approach to evaluation taken in the grandmothers' group was only one of the many possible strategies. Field instructors and students should consider the ways in which their own agency context and funding regulations may influence the evaluation process of groups. Further, evaluation strategies need to be tailored to structural elements, such as the life span of the group. Clearly, a single session group would have a rather simple, worker-developed evaluation strategy. On the other hand, an ongoing group with changing members would have a fairly elaborate evaluation plan, including mechanisms for member involvement. In general terms, planners should insure that the evaluation strategy flows from the group's purpose, and strive for a good fit among all of the elements of the planning process.

Conclusion

The essence of planning is a systematic and comprehensive analysis of a range of factors essential to groups. It includes an understanding of the realities affecting the group and its members, as well as encourages creative thinking about the possibilities available for accomplishing the group's purpose. The following elements of the planning process have been outlined in this chapter to help field instructors and students engage in this enterprise: Agency and social context, Need, Purpose, Composition, Structure, Content, Formation strategy, and Evaluation.

The worksheets following this chapter have been helpful to students and field instructors as they sift through the myriad choices in constructing a plan for a group. Appendix A includes *Work Sheet: Planning Guide for Social Work Groups* which simplifies the process for students and identifies the key elements of a plan. It will be important that each element is considered, and components are adjusted as the plan is generated. Further, students must be prepared to reach for, and hear members' views of the group purpose and how a group should operate. When each section is given attention, the worksheet can become the basis of a proposal, tentatively describing what the group can do, how it can look, and most importantly, what it can accomplish. The contents of a plan and the manner in which it was developed represent part of the student's contribution to the group's contracting process. The worksheet in Appendix B demonstrates the use of the Planning Guide in practice, and has been referred to extensively in this chapter.

This chapter's description of planning effective group assignments, demonstrates how generalist knowledge serves as a platform upon which to build specialized knowledge of pre-group planning with students. The combination of openness and rigor in developing group assignments insures that the planning paradox is put to rest by connecting planning and practice.

References

Bernstein, S. B. (1993).What happened to self-determination? *Social Work with Groups, 16*(1/2), 3-15.

Bertcher, H. J., & Maple, F. (1974). Elements and issues in group composition. In P. Glasser, R. Sarri, & R.Vinter (Eds.), *Individual change through small groups* (pp.180-201). New York: Free Press.

Cohen, C. S. (1995). Making it happen: Building successful support group programs. *Social Work with Groups, 18*(1), 67-80.Cohen, C. S. (1997). The impact of culture in social work practice with groups:The grandmothers as mothers again case study. In E. P. Congress (Ed.), *Multicultural perspectives in working with families* (pp. 311-331). New York: Springer.

Cohen, C. S., & Phillips, M. (1995, October). *Talking about 'not talking': the paradox of confidentiality in groups.* Paper presented at the International Symposium, ssociation for the Advancement of Social Work with Groups. San Diego, CA.

Cohen, C. S., & Pyle, R. (2000). Support groups in the lives of grandparents raising grandchildren. In B. D. Starr (Series Ed.) & C. Cox (Ed.), *To grandmother's house we go, and stay: Perspectives on custodial grandparents* (pp. 235-252). New York: Springer.

Council on Social Work Education. (1994). *Handbook of accreditation standards and procedures* (4th ed.).Alexandria,VA: Council on Social Work Education.

Coyle, G. L. (1948). *Group work with American youth: A guide to the practice of leadership.* New York: Harper.

Falck, H. S. (1988). *Social work:The membership perspective.* New York: Springer.

Garland, J. (1992). Developing and sustaining group work services:A systemic and systematic view. *Social Work with Groups, 15*(4), 89-98.

Germain, C., B., & Gitterman, A. (1996). *The life model of social work practice:Advances in theory and practice* (2nd ed.). New York: Columbia University Press.

Gitterman,A. (1989).Building mutual support in groups. *Social Work with Groups. 12*(2), 5-21.

Glassman, U., & Kates, L. (1988). Strategies for group work field instruction. *Social Work with Groups, 11*(1/2), 111-124.

Glassman, U., & Kates, L. (1990). *Group work: A humanistic approach.* Newbury Park, CA: Sage.

Gutierrez, L. M. (1990). Working with women of color: An empowerment perspective. *Social Work, 35*, 149-153.

Henry, S. (1992). *Group work skills in social work: A four-dimensional approach* (2nd ed.). Pacific Grove, CA: Brooks/Cole.

Knight, C. (1993). A comparison of advanced standing and regular master's students' performance in the second-year field practicum: Field instructors' assessments. *Journal of Social Work Education, 29*, 309-317.

Konopka, G. (1997). The meaning of social group work. In A. S. Alissi & C. G. C. Mergins (Eds.), *Voices from the field: Group work responds* (pp. 3-10). Binghamton, NY: Haworth.

Kurland, R. (1978). Planning: The neglected component of group development. *Social Work with Groups, 1*(2), 173-178.

Kurland, R., & Salmon, R. (1992). Self-determination: Its use and misuse in group work practice and graduate education. In D. F. Fike & B. Rittner (Eds.), *Working from strengths: The essence of group work* (pp.105-121). Miami, FL: Center for Group Work Studies.

Kurland, R., & Salmon, R. (1993). Not one of the gang: Group workers and their role as an authority. *Social Work with Groups, 16*(2), 153-169.

Kurland, R., & Salmon, R. (1998). *Teaching a methods course in social work with groups.* Alexandria, VA: Council on Social Work Education.

Lewis, H. (1982). *The intellectual base of social work practice: Tools for thought in a helping profession.* Binghamton, NY: Haworth.

Magen, R. (1998). Practice with groups. In M. A. Mattaini, C. T. Lowery, & C. H. Meyer (Eds.), *The foundations of social work practice: A graduate text* (2nd ed., pp. 188-208). Washington, DC: NASW Press.

Middleman, R. R., & Goldberg, G. (1972). The concept of structure in experiential learning. In *The annual handbook for group facilitators.* Unpublished manuscript, University of Kentucky at Louisville.

Mondros, J. B., & Wilson, S. M. (1994). *Organizing for power and empowerment.* New York: Columbia University Press.

National Association of Social Workers. (1996). *Code of ethics.* Washington, DC: Author.

Olmstead, M. S. (1959). *The small group.* New York: Random House.

Paradise, R., & Daniels, R. (1973). Group composition as a treatment tool with children. In S. Bernstein (ed.), *Further explorations in group work* (pp. 34-54). Boston: Milford House.

Perlman, H. H. (1979). *Relationship: The heart of helping people.* Chicago: University of Chicago Press.

Pickett, J. P. (Ed.). (2000). *American Heritage Dictionary of the English Language.* Boston: Houghton Mifflin.

Reid, K. E. (1996). *Social work practice with groups: A clinical perspec-*

tive (2nd ed.). Pacific Grove, CA: Brooks/Cole.

Shulman, L. (1971). "Program" in group work: Another look. In W. Schwartz & S. R. Zalba (Eds.), *The practice of group work* (pp. 221-240). New York: Columbia University Press.

Steinberg, D. M. (1997). *The mutual-aid approach to working with groups: Helping people help each other*. Northvale, NJ: Aronson.

Toseland, R. W., & Rivas, R. F. (2001). *An introduction to group work practice* (4th ed.). Needham Heights, MA: Allyn & Bacon.

Tropp, E. (1971). The developmental approach. In Morris, R. (Ed.), The Encyclopedia of Social Work (pp. 1246-1252). New York: NASW Press.

Wayne, J., & Garland, J. (1990). Group work education in the field: The state of the art. *Social Work with Groups, 13*(2), 95-109.

Appendix A

Work Sheet: Planning Guide for Social Work Groups[1]

GROUP NAME: SITE:

GROUP WORKER(S):   START DATE:

1. Agency/SocialContext:

_____

_____

2. Client Need(s):

_____

_____

3. Group Purpose:

_____

_____

4. Group Composition:

_____

_____

5. Group Structure:

_____

_____

_____

6. Group Content:

_____

_____

_____

7. Formation Strategy:

_____

_____

_____

8. Evaluation Strategy:

_____

_____

_____

¹Primarily drawn from: Kurland, R. (1978). Planning: The neglected component of group development. *Social Work with Groups, 1*(2), 173-178.

Appendix B

Work Sheet: Planning Guide for Social Work Groups

GROUP NAME: Grandmothers As Mothers Again Group[1]

SITE: Community Service Center

GROUP WORKER(S): Student Intern & Social Worker

START DATE: Mid-October

1. Agency/Social Context: *Would be a new group for agency, but has had groups for fathers estranged from their children, and runs parenting workshops in Prevention Program. Fits with agency focus on family & vulnerable populations. Idea came from clients in community (fits with need to be responsive). Potential members live close to Community Center (we have contact there). Growing # of grandparents raising grandchildren (3.2 nationally) and more common in our area with parents incarcerated, disabled with AIDS and substance abuse, and grandparents becoming full time care givers, with or without legal custody. Requires no extra outlay of funds; group could raise funds if needed for special activities.*

2. Client Need(s): *Possibly include financial (may have to leave jobs, more expenses, etc.), physical (new tasks and stresses), social (isolation, new milieu, possible ostracism, new family arrangements), informational (new systems to learn and negotiate, advocate for services), emotional (grief as parent, feelings of failure, change of life's plan), etc.*

3. Group Purpose: *To help grandmothers feel supported and more able to cope with raising their grandchildren.*

4. Group Composition: *Grandmothers with responsibility (legal or otherwise) for raising one or more of their grandchildren or great grandchildren due to death or incapacity of child(ren)'s parent(s). Resident of Central City area. Can communicate well in English. Able to travel to group meeting site (wheelchair accessible). Can be self-referred, current client, or referred from other sources.*

5. Group Structure: *Site: Community Service Center, ground floor room outside kitchen; Fees to Members: None; Membership Policy: Open, new members at any time; Frequency: Every two weeks; Meeting Time: During school day with time for travel (time to be determined); Meeting Duration: 2 hours; Duration of Group Life: Open (May break for summer); Decision making: open, structure and content to be further developed by members; Child Care Issues: Infants with grandmothers if necessary (may have babysitting if needed); Meeting notification: Worker to send reminders during initial stage; Outside contacts: Members encouraged to network and contact worker regarding service needs; Worker role: facilitator, enabler, resource gatherer, advocate.*

6. Group Content: *Variable content, expected to include: check-in by members at beginning of meeting, warm-ups & exercises/role-plays, problem sharing and solving discussions brought up by member or worker; speakers or review of materials on topics to be determined by members (e.g., TANF, adoption, schools), advocacy training and/or working with other groups, sharing meals/food, possible opening/closing prayer or ceremony, trips and social activities with or without grandchildren.*

7. Formation Strategy: *Recruitment: flyer to local churches and center, calls to kinship coordinator of child welfare agencies serving area, director's announcement at agency cabinet meetings and at inter-agency and church community council meetings; Screening: telephone or in person contact with all prospective members to assess meeting group membership criteria, initial orientation to group and purpose, gather information about child raising responsibilities among prospective members, discuss best day and time for meeting (within our constraints), assess need for child care during group meeting.*

8. Evaluation Strategy: *Monitor recruitment, sources of membership; Identification of individual expectations at intake and periodic review of expectations and achievement; Process recordings of each meeting and ½ pre-group screening meetings; Weekly supervision re implementation and group progress; Consider pre and periodic administration of social support scale (Zimet et al.1988); Propose group generated scales for social support, stress, group effectiveness, etc.; Develop objectives for student learning, group milestones (e.g., # of members) & member goals with data collection and analysis strategy for each objective.*

---

[1] For more information on this and similar groups, see Cohen, 1997; Cohen, 1995; Cohen & Pyle, 2000.

Chapter 8 | Evaluation and Students' Social Work Practice with Groups

As they move into field work students have a number of questions. These include:

- What am I expected to learn?
- How do I know if I'm learning?
- How do we define success?
- How will we know if we get there?
- How is the group proceeding?
- How do I know if the members' needs are met?

Thinking about these questions directs us towards the complex area of evaluation. In field education students are encouraged to care about their learning and about what they are accomplishing with clients. They are expected to understand their professional function, their goals and achievements, and to monitor changes in the group and its members. In a parallel process, group members may also wonder about their place in the group and think about what they are doing and achieving. Finally field instructors may well have these same questions as they begin to supervise group work practice, form relationships with students, try to assess what has been learned, and by implication their own success as educators.

For some field instructors, encountering the student questions listed above is enough to raise anxiety about how students and groups are progressing. These instructors experience the questions as a test of mentorship. Other field instructors may rejoice when students raise them, welcoming the opportunity to assess their students' performance and group outcomes. Regardless of initial reactions, these questions must be answered through a thoughtful evaluation process. Field settings provide an ideal environment for students to learn about their own performance and about assessment of their group work practice.

This chapter's primary purpose is to provide an overview of student and group evaluation, and a discussion of commonly used tools in a field evaluation. First, sources of support for professional attention to evaluation will be identified, and then challenges to implementation will be examined.

Orientation to Evaluation in Social Work

On the broadest level, the social work profession mandates evaluation through the Code of Ethics of the National Association of Social Workers (1996). The Code directs social workers to consider the study of our work, client outcomes, and the practice environment as essential to competent practice. In sum, the Code directs professional social workers to:

- Monitor and evaluate policies, the implementation of pro-grams, and practice interventions.

- Promote and facilitate evaluation and research to contribute to the development of knowledge.

- Critically examine and keep current with emerging knowl-edge relevant to social work.

- Fully use evaluation and research evidence in their profes-sional practice.

- Continually strive to increase their professional knowledge and skills.

- Aspire to contribute to the knowledge base of the profession.

Focus on practice evaluation is further mandated by the Council on Social Work Education (CSWE) in their expectations of competence upon graduation. Students successfully completing baccalaureate programs are expected to be able to "evaluate their own practice interventions and those of other relevant systems under supervision" (CSWE, 1994, B5.7.8). Graduates of masters programs in social work should be able to "conduct empirical evaluations of their own practice interventions and those of other relevant systems" (M5.7.11).

In regard to practice with groups, the Association for the Advancement of Social Work with Groups (AASWG) addresses the centrality of assessment in their Practice Standards (AASWG, 1999) by directing workers to monitor and evaluate how successful groups are in accomplishing their objectives. The Association proposes observation and measurement of outcomes, processes, or both as study methods. While evaluation of social work with groups has not been center stage in the literature, strategies for evaluating such practice have been available for at least fifty years (Trecker, 1955). The current call for all social workers to engage in empirically based practice has increased attention to assessment of group processes and outcomes as well as goal achievement of individual members (Anderson, 1987; Magen, 1998).

Evaluation is integral to fulfilling the multiple roles and responsibilities of field instructors. First, field instructors must evaluate student performance, group outcomes, and client goal achievement in their role of gatekeeper, insuring that inappropriate and poorly skilled students do not graduate into the profession. Second, as administrators of students' learning experience, field instructors are empowered by educational institutions to implement assignments and monitor students' progress with groups in the agency environment. Third, as teachers, field instructors must work towards understanding what they are teaching and what students are learning. Finally, as career socializers (Middleman & Rhodes, 1985), field instructors guide students to develop and apply the principles, values, and ethics of the profession in their practice. The responsibilities of this role extend beyond the immediate field placement, requiring field instructors to prepare students for work in any social work capacity and to instill commitment to continuing knowledge development and evaluation of practice.

Field instruction and the supervisory relationship are built around the expectation of constructive assessment leading to greater learning. During the process of forging a professional self, most students are intensely curious about what they are doing and whether they are making a difference in the lives of clients. Furthermore, they are subject to an increased emphasis on accountability. They should enter field education and professional practice with the expectation that evaluation will be an integral component of the learning process.

Challenges to Evaluation

Given the aforementioned supportive conditions, one would expect a strong focus on evaluation in field education. However, assessment of student performance remains an area of difficulty for many field instructors (Bogo & Vayda, 1998), and there is limited evidence of widespread student activity in the area of group work evaluation

(Galinsky, Turnbull, Meglin, & Wilner, 1993; Knight, 1999). If it is true that evaluation helps us identify and understand what and how we are doing (Parsons, Jorgenson, & Hernandez, 1994), perhaps we should explore the reasons why we resist finding out.

Possible obstacles to evaluation include those lodged in the agency and the supervisory relationship. At the agency level, Weissman (1987) points out that while feedback is essential to organizations in the long run, it can be quite dysfunctional in the short run. Negative feedback can create what Kadushin (1992) refers to as "psychic debris," fall-out generated by angry feelings. For the same reasons, examination of what students are doing and how clients are faring in groups may initially challenge the working relationship field instructors have struggled to establish with their students.

When students talk about practice evaluation, their discussion is often peppered with words such as "risk" and "opportunity," echoing words used by clients when approaching difficult work (Compton & Galaway, 1999). Perhaps clients' parallel phenomenon of ambivalence is useful in understanding how students are of two minds when approaching evaluation. Students understand that there is a great deal to be learned through assessment of their performance and the work of the group, just as clients recognize the benefits of their involvement in the evaluation process. Students however, like clients, can also see the inherent risks in examining what they are doing. These risks include challenges to a student's sense of self, the status quo of the field placement, or the field instructor–student relationship.

Adding to the complexity of evaluation is the recognition that there is not always a direct relationship between student performance and group outcomes. Students can sadly discover that in spite of feeling good about a group meeting, they may not be helping the members to move toward agreed upon goals. On the other hand, just because clients do not fully achieve what they intended does not necessarily mean that students' learning or performance was not at a high level. It is also possible for students' skilled interventions not to be reflected in group and member achievement.

Contracting at the onset of field instruction around goals and the assessment strategies used to measure progress towards them will help in overcoming obstacles and will model appropriate practice with clients (Fox & Zischka, 1982). The collaboration between student and field instructor is constructed through working together on developing, implementing, and evaluating group work assignments. Mutual goal setting and subsequent evaluation of process and outcome will lead to genuine partnership in supervision, just as it does in practice. As

Shulman (1994) points out: "Teaching cannot be conceived of as simply handing over knowledge or covering the agenda" (p. 5). In field education, a reciprocal relationship is forged in which both student and supervisor monitor and evaluate the learning processes and client outcomes.

Framework for Evaluation

Several questions arise for field instructors embarking on evaluation of students. These include:

- How is the student doing as the worker with the group?
- What is the nature of the group's process and goal achievement?
- What progress is being made towards achieving each member's goals and outcomes?

These three questions, suggesting areas of inquiry, can be followed by two more questions, focused on strategies, as field instructors evaluate student work with groups in the field:

- How will I engage in an evaluation partnership to discover the answers to these questions?
- What tools and instruments are available for use in the evaluation enterprise?

Together, these five questions form a framework proposed for assessing students' group work practice. The first three questions address three key areas for evaluation: (1) student performance, (2) group process and goal achievement, and (3) member outcome. The fourth question locates evaluation within the supervisory relationship, a partnership of unrivaled intensity in professional practice that is focused on accountability (Kolevzon, 1979). The fifth question suggests the means for finding answers about performance, processes, and outcomes with the introduction of data collection techniques.

The remainder of this chapter will discuss the three areas for evaluation in greater detail with recommendations for supervisory approaches and assessment tools in each area. Many of the instruments and strategies described in this chapter may already be familiar, and are commonly used to document student work. However, evaluation goes beyond identifying student activities and describing interventions. These tools can be enlisted in evaluation-related activities only when the data they generate is purposefully analyzed in relation to the goals and objectives for student, group-level, and client-level outcomes.

Evaluation of Student Performance

Field instructors and students are most familiar with this area of evaluation, focusing on the activities and interventions of students. In some way, evaluation of student performance is the sine qua non of field education. The very phrases we use to describe the process of student learning in field education, such as:"tutoring the professional self" and "refining the instrument" suggest that students undergo dramatic changes through learning about themselves and the impact of services on clients. However, just because evaluation of performance is expected and necessary, it is not necessarily easy.

Two key conditions must be present for successful evaluation of student performance. First, the student must be able to tolerate criticism at a time of particular vulnerability. As discussed in Chapter 6, tuning into the student's state of mind and phase of learning can help field instructors form a helpful alliance. Students in the earliest stages are most in need of and most vulnerable to feedback since they are not in a position to assess their own performance. Field instructors should frame evaluative comments using solid social work practice strategies, including the use of the strengths perspective. In addition, educationally grounded discussion of the supervisory relationship can be very helpful in modeling practice-based evaluation, particularly once the student has had some success with group assignments (Shulman, 1994).

The second essential condition for evaluation is the field instructor's ability to tolerate challenges to their supervisory input with students. As we have learned from our own experience, evaluation is something that can get easier with time, but never completely loses its potential to sting. It is important to acknowledge that field instructors will have varying degrees of difficulty with evaluation, and it is possible (and often useful) to discuss this directly with students in ways that model effective practice partnerships and the conscious use of self (Webb, 1988).

Process recordings. Chief among the large number of existing evaluation tools that can be used to assess student performance in field instruction is the process recording, a verbatim account of a session's events that also can include students' preparation, feelings, and reflections. Process recordings are multipurpose tools, since they provide data to evaluate the work of individual members, the group as a whole, and the interventions of students. While there has been controversy about the utility of such a widely applicable tool (Dwyer& Urbanowski, 1966; Fox & Gutheil, 2000), there is near universal agreement that process recordings are the primary mechanism to bring the group experience to life for the field instructors' review (Urdang, 1979). Chapter 5 discusses this tool and its importance in group work practice and provides several process recording structures. Analyzing the content of these recordings in single sessions and over time for specific themes and goal achievements make them highly valuable tools for evaluation.

Field evaluation forms. The field evaluation form provided by the social work program is central to the evaluation of student performance. Such documents are generally designed broadly, allowing for a wide range of student assignments and agency settings (Wilson, 1981). Since each educational program develops its own questions and format for these evaluations, some evaluation forms may be more suited to reports about skills learned through group work than others. This broad approach makes it easy to focus on particular aspects of students' work in the field, while overlooking others. Suffice it to say that group work assignments should be considered in any overall evaluation of students' progress. Faculty advisors or field education staff can generally assist in helping field instructors make standardized forms as relevant as possible to particular students' experiences.

Inventories of group work skill. There are tools for measuring students' skills that have been specifically constructed for work with groups. For example, Dies & MacKenzie (1983) have developed the *Worker Self-Evaluation Group Leadership Skills Scale,* in which students read statements and mark responses that best fit their skill level or situation. Each question begins with the phrase: "In this group I..." and then provides numbered choices to fill in the rest of the sentence such as "notice who talks to whom," "act assertively," "stick to the topic," "invite feedback," or "demonstrate acceptance." Such a tool could be individually tailored to particular students. In fact, the development of the assessment tool itself can be a valuable area of discussion in supervision, since the assessment tool highlights both generalist and specific skills used in group assignments and supports commitment to practice evaluation.

Narrative approaches are also useful in identifying students' skills in group work practice. Glassman and Kates (1988) propose such an approach, suggesting that field instructors ask students to tell the story of a group session to bring students' interventions into supervision for examination. Field instructors can build on students' reminiscences of group experiences and heighten self-awareness in three ways:

- Raising specific questions, such as: How do you think group members perceive you in the worker role? How do you usually handle yourself in an authority position?

- Providing feedback, modeling the "I perceive" and "I feel" form of expression

- Encouraging fantasy, especially when students are reluctant to confront particular group situations or engage particular group members and asking "what if?" questions can help students enter into unknown or fearful situations by capturing their essences (p. 119)

These strategies use students' recall of what happened to evaluate their practice and the group's achievement.

Competencies and experiences with groups must be considered in light of expectations for learning and the purpose of assignments for students and clients. Responses and stories generated through these approaches serve as quantitative and qualitative findings for analysis in the evaluation of student performance. These findings are then considered in light of students' previous experience and competencies as well as learning goals and purposes of particular assignments.

Evaluation of Group Process and Outcome

Simply evaluating students' interventions is meaningless without assessment of what is happening in the group as a whole. It is by looking at the group experience that supervision can focus on what students are doing and the impact of students' and members' actions. Evaluation of practice at the group level is generally divided between assessment strategies that examine group process and those that examine group outcome (Garvin, 1997; Toseland & Rivas, 2001; Zastrow, 1997). This distinction is used to clarify the difference between these evaluative targets, since many students tend to blend the two together. In essence, "process" refers to how groups operate and "outcome" refers to what groups accomplish in relation to their purposes. As discussed in earlier chapters, clear boundaries between process and outcome are often artificial, since they continually affect each other. For example, the process of building cohesion and mutual aid will have implications for group outcomes, especially when a group's purpose is to create a supportive environment for members facing common challenges. However, distinctions are useful during the evaluation process, since they open each to review and analysis and direct students and field instructors to consider both process and outcome as key areas of attention.

Diagrammatic assessments of group process. The old saying that a picture is worth a thousand words may be true in relation to identifying and evaluating group process. Diagrams such as the sociogram (Cartwright & Zander, 1968) depict the transactions between group members, and the relationships that link them together; these diagrams can also include observations on seating arrangements as well as the feelings of closeness, conflict, and identification among members. A similar tool that most social work students are familiar with is the Eco-map (Hartman, 1978), which can be employed in work with individuals, families, groups, and communities. The Eco-map is a paper and pencil drawing, constructed by students alone, by students and group members, or by students and field instructors that can depict the relative strength and quality of relationships among all group participants, the group and the outside environment, or both.

Diagrammatic strategies provide simple, but comprehensive pictures of group dynamics at a moment in time. Particularly useful when students need new perspectives on group dynamics, sociograms, Eco-maps, and similar illustrations provide unique snapshots, and can potentially be used to bring group members into the evaluative process. This technique has recently been adopted for data collection in research, because of its power to present a great deal of information about how clients see their relationships (Harold, Mercier, & Colaross, 1997). When constructed at intervals through the life of groups, diagrams can provide a history of group process and development. While not necessary, a form can be provided, or it can be constructed spontaneously with materials at hand. Figure 1 suggests one way to identify group members and their relationships inside and outside the group.

Measurements of Group Achievement. While most often used with individuals and families, goal attainment scaling may be a useful technique for evaluating and tracking the achievement of the group as a whole (Kiresuk & Sherman, 1968). Originally designed under a contract with the National Institutes of Mental Health, it can be used to look at a group's degree of success in meeting its goals. This technique also provides data on what the group feels is important, and their measures of success. Goal attainment scaling works well with a problem-solving (Brown, 1991) or task-oriented approach (Reid & Epstein, 1978) since it challenges members to define the group purpose and how they would know that it had been achieved.

The core of goal attainment scaling is the clear articulation of goals, followed by identification of expected levels of achievement. A written form is considered useful, since it provides a document for future study. Students can become familiar with this technique by using it to identify and monitor their own learning goals, in dialogue with field instructors. The process of creating the form in supervision parallels

Figure 1
GROUP ECO-MAP

Group Name: Date Completed:

Worker:

Person(s) Creating Eco-map:

Instructions

Fill in connections where they exist. Indicate nature of connections with a descriptive word or by drawing different kinds of lines: ——— for strong, -------- for tenuous, +++ for stressful. Draw arrows along lines to signify flow of energy, resources, etc. Identify significant people and systems, filling in empty circles as needed.

Key: M=Member(Identify), W=Worker, A=Agency, C=Community, F=Family, O=Other (Identify)

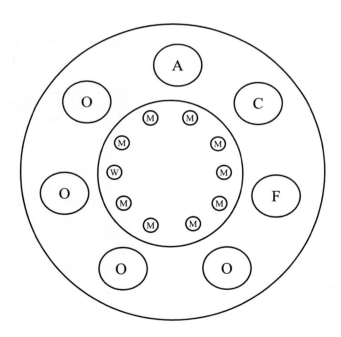

the process of contracting with the group, and can prepare students for that challenge. Since it provides a focus on overall group goals, students can use it early in group assignments to plan for how they will help the members forge a collective purpose without ignoring members' individual needs. In addition, goal attainment scaling can be used at the end of a group's life, and used to compare achievements between groups (Flowers & Booarem, 1989). Field instructors can use the form to evaluate students' knowledge, progress, and areas for learning. Subsequent use of the form will inform students, field instructors, and members about how the group is doing in reaching its desired outcomes. A template that can be adapted as needed is presented in Figure 2.

Reid and Epstein (1978) have developed a similar method for assessing the degree to which group members or leaders have accomplished agreed upon tasks. This strategy begins with an inventory of separate tasks or activities that have been selected by members as important to the achievement of the group as a whole. Tasks and time frames are assigned to particular members. Members and workers periodically rate the degree to which each agreed-upon task has been completed. The use of a five point scale (as shown in Figure 2), provides quantitative data for analysis that isolates results from other variables such as effort, intentions, or motivation.

Group summaries including process and outcome. A simple summary recording form can be used that asks about both process and outcome with four questions:

- What were the student's plans?
- What did the group do?
- How did the group operate?
- What are the student's impressions and future plans?

A more detailed approach to evaluating group process and outcome comes from the recording outline developed by Grace Coyle and the American Association of Group Workers Committee (Trecker, 1955). Their suggested format, still remarkably fresh, included the following questions:

- What has been happening to the individuals in the group?
- How has the group changed in purpose and membership?
- How do members relate to each other?
- How is the group governed?

Figure 2

GOAL ATTAINMENT WORKSHEET

Name of Group: Date Completed:

Worker:

Group Purpose/Mission:

	Goal A:	Goal B:	Goal C:
Much more than expected result (5)			
More than expected result (4)			
Expected or most likely result (3)			
Less than expected result (2)			
Much less than expected result (1)			

- How does the group make up its mind?
- What about esprit de corps?
- What are the dominant values in the group?
- What has been the program of the group?
- What is the relationship of the group to other groups?
- What is the relationship of the worker to members of the group?

Developed over 40 years later, the following Summary, Observation, Developmental Stage, and Assessment (SODA) summary recording form (Cohen & Garrett, 1995) also explores process and outcome, focusing on the special aspects of social work practice with groups (see Figure 3). Discussion of the SODA form itself in supervision can be useful to identify distinctive elements of groups, and direct students to focus on these phenomena.

Cohen and Garrett (1995) point out that the form assumes that students and field instructors are familiar with group work concepts. When knowledge of group work practice is limited, it may be difficult to understand and use the form, compromising its value. However, some gaps in knowledge of group work practice can be filled through this volume and through suggested resources in chapter 9.

The danger with the evaluation strategies presented and other strategies for evaluating the group as a whole is that if group goals are erroneously conceptualized, task completion and group vitality may have little correlation to the accomplishment of the group's overall purposes or resolution of clients' concerns. Therefore, development of an evaluation strategy must begin at the earliest possible stage in planning for groups. As discussed in chapter 7, exploration of clients' needs and the service environment should be followed by tentative formulation of group purposes to which members, students, and field instructors can subscribe. Next, field instructors and students should formulate ideas regarding group structure, content, and pre-group formation. Along with this, plans for evaluation should be made. As data on process and outcome is generated, it must be analyzed in relation to what groups set out to do, and the extent to which they reach their goals.

Evaluation of Member Outcome

Field instructors and students may be familiar with this third area of evaluation, since assessment of individual client outcomes is commonly discussed in classrooms and agencies. Ultimately, groups are made up of individuals, and the achievement of individual goals through

Figure 3

GROUP PROCESS RECORD

Group: Date:

Group Worker:

Group description

Group purpose and goals:

Time limited or openended:

Session number:

Group members present (include seating arrangement using arrows to indicate communication flow):

S.O.D.A. Recording

Summary of group content:

Observation of group processes:

Norms:

Roles:

Communication patterns:

Group cohesion/attraction/mutual aid:

Developmental stage:

Assessment of practice (critique of worker's interventions, questions, comments):

the group process is an important area of study. As Garvin (1997) states, members have a right to examine whether their investment in the group work process has attained their goals (p. 191). Some of the tools already discussed, such as Goal Attainment Scaling and the Eco-map, are routinely used with individuals. Given the wide variety of techniques available, only those for practice with groups will be discussed in this section.

Postmeeting feedback strategies. The perceptions of members regarding the functioning of the group, the performance of the worker, and their own goal achievement on a sessional basis can be invaluable to student learning. Individual member feedback can be built into every group session or occur at intervals to be determined by the participants. Collection mechanisms can range from a simple question asking what members felt was accomplished at a particular meeting to an extended review of members' expectations, relative achievement, and revised goals. A middle ground is suggested in the postgroup questionnaire drawn from Rose (1984), and presented in Figure 4.

Postgroup assessments by members. When groups draw to a close, it often seems that the last thing members (and workers) want to do is evaluate their progress. However, students should be encouraged to resist the urge to escape from evaluation, since closure includes the identification of what has been achieved relative to members' goals for the group experience. It is important that this process of reflection be shared collectively by those who were a part of the group. This can take the form of group discussion, guided by the student with an eye on insuring that all members participate to the extent possible.

Zastrow (1997) proposes using a simple, anonymous questionnaire that can be completed by group members at the final session, or afterward by mail if necessary. He cautions that responses will be affected by the mood of members, and more dissatisfied members are less likely to complete questionnaires than satisfied members, particularly when the surveys are administered by mail. However, the opportunity for members to reflect on and share their own assessment of their achievements and struggles in the group must be provided as part of ethical professional practice. Group discussions and individual surveys are techniques to meet this standard.

In some group settings, structured activities may provide formats for the assessment of individual outcomes. For example, members can create a group poem about the experience, including a line by each member. Students can suggest the line begin with the words: "In the beginning of this group I was ..." and end with "And now at the end I

Figure 4

POST-SESSION QUESTIONNAIRE

Group: Date:

Member:

1. How useful was today's session?

  Circle One: High/Very Somewhat A Little Not at All

2. What was your involvement today?

3. Rate the extent of your self-disclosure of relevant information

  Circle One: High/Very Somewhat A Little Not at All

4. How important to you were the problems or situations you or others discussed?

5. How would you best describe the interrelationships among members and leaders in this group?

6. Circle all words best describing you at today's session.

  excited   bored   depressed   interested
  anxious   involved   holding back comfortable

7. How satisfied were you with today's session?

am...." While this strategy draws upon the individual evaluations of members, it weaves them together to form a statement from the group as a whole.

Conclusion

This chapter has focused on evaluating students' group work practice in three areas: student performance, group process and goal achievement, and member outcome. A variety of assessment approaches useful within the supervisory relationship, and tools that can be used for data collection in group settings have also been covered. We have identified that student performance and group process are relevant to group and member achievements. By identifying phenomena of both the group as a whole and individual members as areas for evaluation, field instructors convey the importance of both levels of inquiry and the interrelationship between members and the group (Brower & Rose, 1989; Glisson, 1987).

It is hoped that this discussion will help field instructors fulfill their mandate to incorporate evaluation as a central part of their supervisory agenda. While challenges to evaluation are formidable, field instructors must find ways to address fears of exposure and overcome resistance because the rewards are substantial. Benefits include increased self-awareness and expanded skill for all participants, including students, clients, and field instructors. Field instructors will find that the supervisory relationship is the ideal vehicle for evaluation since it presents a model of the collaboration expected between workers and clients in groups. Paralleling the role of the social worker in practice, Miller (1985) suggests that "the merely knowledgeable supervisor gives advice; the wise one is more knowing than telling, listens and depends on the work as a source of insight into the worker"(p. 752). By bringing evaluation into the mainstream of social work in the field experience, field instructors induct students into a lifetime of sound, empirically-based group work practice.

References

Anderson, J. D. (1987). Integrating research and practice in social work with groups. *Social Work with Groups, 9*(3), 111-123.

Association for the Advancement of Social Work in Groups. (1999). *Standards for social work practice with groups.* Akron, OH: Author.

Bogo, M., & Vayda, E. (1998). *The practice of field instruction in social work: Theory and practice.* New York: Columbia University Press.

Brower, A. M., & Rose, S. D. (1989). The group work research dilemma. *Journal of Social Science Research, 13*(2), 1-8.

Brown, L. (1991). *Groups for growth and change*. New York: Longman.

Cartwright, D., & Zander, A. (1968). *Group Dynamics*. New York: Harper and Row.

Cohen, M. B., & Garrett, K. J. (1995). Helping field instructors become more effective group work educators. *Social Work with Groups, 18*(2/3), 135-148.

Compton, B., & Galaway, B. (1999). *Social work processes*. Pacific Grove: Brooks/Cole.

Council on Social Work Education. (1994). *Handbook of accreditation standards and procedures* (4th ed.). Alexandria, VA: Author.

Dies, R., & MacKenzie, K. (1983). *Advances in group psychotherapy: Integrating research and practice*. New York: International Universities Press.

Dwyer, M., & Urbanowski, M. (1966). Student process recording: A plea for structure. *Social Casework, 46*(5), 284-286.

Flowers, J. V., & Booarem, C. D. (1989). Four studies toward an empirical foundation for group therapy. *Journal of Social Service Research. 13* (2), 105-121.

Fox, R., & Gutheil, I. A. (2000). Process recording: A means for conceptualizing and evaluating practice. *Journal of Teaching in Social Work, 20*(1/2), 39-55.

Fox, R., & Zischka, P. C. (1982). Using goal-focused contracts in supervision. *Social Work in Education, 4*(3), 16-27.

Galinsky, M. J., Turnbull, J. E., Meglin, D. E., & Wilner, M. E. (1993). Confronting the reality of collaborative practice research: Issues of practice, design, measurement, and team development. *Social Work, 38*, 440-449.

Garvin, C. D. (1997). *Contemporary group work*. Needham Heights, MA: Allyn & Bacon.

Glassman, U., & Kates, L. (1988). Strategies for group work field instruction. *Social Work with Groups, 11*(1/2), 111-124.

Glisson, C. (1987). The group versus the individual as the unit of analysis in small group research. *Social Work with Groups, 9*(3), 15-30.

Harold, R. D., Mercier, L. R., & Colarossi, L. G. (1997). Eco maps: A tool to bridge the practice-research gap. *Journal of Sociology and Social Welfare, 24*(4), 29-44.

Hartman, A. (1978). Diagramic assessment of family relationships. *Social Casework, 59*, 465-476.

Kadushin, A. (1992). *Supervision in social work*. New York: Columbia University Press.

Kiresuk, T. J., & Sherman, R. E. (1968). Goal attainment scaling: A general method for evaluating comprehensive community mental health programs. *Community Mental Health Journal, 4*(6), 443-453.

Knight, C. (1999). A study of MSW and BSW students' involvement with group work in the field practicum. *Social Work with Groups, 20*(2), 31-49.

Kolevzon, M. (1979). Evaluating the supervisory relationship in field placements. *Social Work, 24*, 241-244.

Magen, R. (1998). Practice with groups. In M. A. Mattaini, C. T. Lowery, & C. H. Meyer (Eds.), *The foundations of social work practice: A graduate text* (2nd ed., pp. 188-208). Washington, DC: NASW Press. Middleman, R. R., & Rhodes, G. B. (1985). Competent supervision: Making imaginative judgments. Englewood Cliffs, NJ: Prentice-Hall.

Miller, I. (1985). Supervision. In Anne Minahan (Ed.-in-Chief), *Encyclopedia of social work* (18th ed., pp. 748-756). New York: National Association of Social Workers.

National Association of Social Workers. (1996, 1998). *Code of ethics.* Washington, DC: Author.

Parsons, R. J., Jorgensen, J. D., & Hernandez, S. H. (1994). *The integration of social work practice*. Pacific Grove, CA: Brooks/Cole.

Reid, W., & Epstein, L. (1978). *Task-centered practice*. New York: Columbia University Press.

Rose, S. D. (1984). Use of data in identifying and resolving group problems in goal-oriented treatment groups. *Social Work with Groups, 7*(2), 23-26.

Shulman, L. (1994). *Teaching the helping skills: A field instructor's guide* (2nd ed.). Alexandria, VA: Council on Social Work Education.

Toseland, R. W., & Rivas, R. F. (2001). *An introduction to group work practice* (4th ed.). Neeedham Heights, MA: Allyn & Bacon.

Trecker, H. B. (1955). *Social group work: Principles and practices*. New York: Whitside.

Urdang, E. (1979). In defense of process recording. *Smith College Studies in Social Work, 50*(1), 1-15.

Webb, N. B. (1988). The role of the field instructor in the socialization of students. *Social Casework, 69*(1), 35-40.

Weissman, H. H. (1987). Planning for client feedback: Content and context. *Administration in Social Work, 11*(3/4), 205-221.

Wilson, S. J. (1981). *Field instruction: Techniques for supervisors*. New York: Free Press.

Zastrow, C. (1997). *Social work with groups: Using the class as a group leadership laboratory* (4th ed.). Chicago: Nelson-Hall.

Chapter 9 | Where to from Here?

Any one volume can go just so far! In order to remain expert as a field instructor of group work practice, it is necessary to continually reinforce and augment the content this book has offered. Therefore, the authors conclude with suggestions for ongoing development as an educator of group work practice in the field. Some of the suggestions have been identified in chapter 5 in relation to the education of students. Many of these approaches are equally helpful for the educator.

Avenues for Continued Learning

Students

Field instructors can ask their students to bring into supervision all classroom syllabi and bibliographies that refer to group work content. This material will include updated literature reflecting the latest developments in practice and research. Field instructors should also ask students to identify the concepts from the literature and class discussions that seem most salient to their field experiences. Such discussions are helpful to both field instructors and students as they relate theory to practice, and provide opportunity to critically examine the thoughts and contributions of perceived experts in the field.

Social Work Programs

Social work programs never lose sight of the fact that agencies and field instructors voluntarily devote their time to help educate their students. Most programs welcome the opportunity to offer educational experiences to field instructors and agencies as a way to thank them for their contributions. In fact, social work programs often feel frustrated about the low numbers of field instructors who take advantage of the workshops and other educational opportunities they offer.

Do not hesitate to ask for consultation about the student's practice from the assigned faculty liaison or through him/her, from any other qualified faculty member. Programs may respond by providing at least a single session consultation to an individual, or to a group of staff. If the demand warrants, the program could also organize a seminar or workshop on group work for field instructors from several settings. Your student's program will probably be heartened by your interest and motivation to provide the best education you can to their students.

Colleagues

A regularly scheduled peer group meeting to review group work practice is a valuable structure for continuing education in group work practice, and is also consistent with the expectations of professional life. Professionals within the same discipline are expected to be accountable to each other (Schein, 1972), and adult education principles emphasize the value of peers learning from each other (Brannon, 1985). The benefits of peer group consultation are similar to many of those of group supervision as described in Chapter 5. Peer support also contributes to the fight against burnout during these stressful times for most social work practitioners (Freudenberger, 1981).

Outside Consultation

If your agency does not have a staff member with specialized knowledge in social work with groups, it can hire an outside consultant for the expertise he/she can bring. Consultation is an efficient way to capitalize on a professional's specialized knowledge (Rieman, 1992). Consultation could be arranged on a regular basis or as needed. It can focus on generalized practice issues or on specific practice problems as they arise. In any case, the perspective of someone from the outside can provide valuable information and stimulation to any agency, and can help raise awareness of factors within the agency that may be impeding the development of efficient and effective group work service (see chapter 3).

Literature on Group Work Practice

No professional should underestimate how helpful written materials can be. Students report on the high value of professional literature and on their ability to independently apply concepts they have read about to their practice with groups (Wayne & Richards, 1996). It is in the best interest of any agency to develop a library of professional literature to which any staff member can refer. Many basic and specialized group work books and articles cited in this work would be valuable additions to such a library. The journal *Social Work With Groups* is an especially good resource for the latest developments and trends in social work practice with groups. Online journals and websites of organizations can lead you to additional resources.

Professional Organizations

Professional organizations play an invaluable role in bringing together people with similar interests for educational and political purposes. The Association for the Advancement of Social Work With Groups was organized in the 1970s by professionals who feared the movement toward generalist practice would lead to a loss of expertise in social work with groups. In addition to its political purpose of maintaining a commitment to high standards of group work practice, it also has played a major educational role in providing a forum for the exchange of ideas, experiences, and knowledge about the method. Joining such an organization provides members with opportunities for regional and international conferences, and facilitates access to relevant journals and other publications.

Conferences

Usually one does not have to be a member of a professional organization to attend its conference. Be on the lookout for conferences or conference sessions that focus on groups. The opportunity to interact with people from a range of settings will bring fresh perspectives.

Continuing Education Courses

Organizations such as the National Association of Social Workers or the continuing education departments of schools of social work in your area may offer seminars, workshops, or courses on social work practice with groups. When you need to earn continuing education units for licensure or certification, consider seeking out experiences that focus on group work practice.

Your Own Experiences

Most professionals in agency practice feel extremely busy and pressured. There is little time for reflection or a systematic study of one's practice. In addition, most practitioners are "doers" who prefer practice itself, rather than the labor-intensive task of voluntarily keeping records for their own educational purposes. Yet, all that we have said about the value of recording process for students applies to field instructors as well. According to Bertha Reynolds (1942), experienced practitioners are able to use their "observing ego" to guide them in their own quest for continuing growth. The teaching tools recommended for students in chapters 5 and 8 are invaluable in making one's own practice that much more observable. Process recordings, tapes (audio and audio/visual), and the combined use of these are helpful to all who wish to "supervise" themselves.

Group Members

We have already discussed the value to members in being active participants in an evaluation process of their group experience (Chapter 8). Their feedback to you as worker about how they cexperienced the group and your work with it can teach a good deal about how to proceed in the future.

Conclusion

According to Erickson (1963), young adults face the challenge of remaining open to the "inspiration of teachers" and to the new ideas and perspectives they offer. There is the danger upon reaching adulthood of feeling "fully developed, " and no longer in need of continuing growth and development. That danger also exists as one reaches the adulthood of professional life. Both Erickson and Reynolds (1942) agree that it is through the process of passing on one's knowledge and wisdom to the next generation that the teacher continues to be a lifelong learner. We hope this book and its suggestions support your innate desire to become an increasingly effective educator and strengthens your commitment to teaching social work practice with groups.

References

Brannon, D. (1985). Adult learning principles and methods for enhancing the training role of supervisors. *The Clinical Supervisor*, *3*(2), 27-41.

Erickson, E. H. (1963). *Childhood and society* (2nd ed.). New York: W.W. Norton.

Freudenberger, H. (1981). *Burn out: How to beat the high cost of success*. New York: Double Day.

Rieman, D. (1992). *Strategies in social work consultation*. White Plains, NY: Longman.

Reynolds, B. (1942). *Learning and teaching in the practice of social work*. New York: Russell & Russell.

Schein E. (1972). *Professional education: Some new directions*. New York: McGraw-Hill.

Wayne, J., & Richards, M. (1996, October). *Group work education: The student perspective*. Paper presented at the 18th Annual Symposium on Social Work with Groups, Ann Arbor, MI.

Index